Publis‍ Tutor Master Services

David Malindine
B.A.(Hons), M.A.(London), P.G.C.E.,
Adv.Dip.Ed.(Open), R.S.A. Cert.

Tutor Master Services
61 Ashness Gardens
Greenford
Middlesex
UB6 0RW
david@tutormaster-services.co.uk
www.tutormaster-services.co.uk

Acknowledgements

Thanks to Christine Malindine for preparing this book,

to Ruth Sladden for kindly proofreading the scripts

and to Mary Walton for her contributions and advice.

For

Doug and Jeffo

Joe and Jack

Other books by the Tutor Master

Tutor Master helps you Write Stories Book One
(Published 2004, 2nd edition 2007) ISBN: 978-0-9555909-0-0

Tutor Master helps you Write Stories Book Two
(Published 2007)   ISBN: 978-0-9555909-1-7

Who this book is for

An important aim in writing this book has been to provide an accessible, user-friendly reference to assist all those who wish to improve their knowledge and understanding of the English language, English literature and literacy.

It is ideal for school, college and university students of all ages.

It will assist parents who wish to further their own knowledge of English and who may wish to give greater guidance and support to their children and their studies.

It will help those who are learning English by providing key words to improve literacy and understanding of English.

As a handy and easy to use reference book, it will serve as a useful resource for teachers and for lecturers in colleges and universities.

This book will be particularly useful for students and teachers in language schools and TEFL colleges.

How to use this book

Over 500 words are listed in alphabetical order.

For some words which are difficult to pronounce a phonetic cue is provided to help pronunciation. For more clarity, Tutor Master suggests visiting dictionary or encyclopaedia websites that provide voice pronunciation of the required word, so that the word can be heard.

A definition is given for each of the words listed and in many cases examples are provided.

Where it is considered appropriate for ease of reference, words that are linked to definitions found elsewhere in the book are underlined.

Where brief examples are given they are written in italics but other examples are shown in grey boxes.

All examples and poems are by the Tutor Master except where the origins are unknown or are otherwise credited.

ABBREVIATION (ab-reev-ee-a-shun) The shortening of a <u>word</u> to fewer <u>letters</u> or just the initials, to represent the whole word. Sometimes the letters are separated by <u>full stop</u>s.

The generally accepted rule about using a full stop with an abbreviation relates to where the word has been cut. It is more common to write abbreviations **with** full stops if the point at which the word has been cut is in the middle of the word.

Professor	⟹	*Prof.*
Abbreviation	⟹	*Abbrev.*
February	⟹	*Feb.*
Anonymous	⟹	*Anon.*

If the word has been abbreviated by leaving out the middle and putting only the first/first few and last letters, full stops are not usually included.

Doctor	⟹	*Dr*
Road	⟹	*Rd*
Avenue	⟹	*Ave*
Department	⟹	*Dept*

ABSTRACT NOUN (See Noun.)

ACCENT (ack-sent) The different ways that a spoken <u>language</u> is pronounced. Accents vary from region to region.

ACRONYM (ack-ro-nim) An <u>abbreviation</u> where the initial <u>letters</u> make a real <u>word</u>, e.g. *GOSH* (*G*reat *O*rmond *S*treet *H*ospital).

Sometimes an acronym is made from <u>syllable</u>s or parts of words, e.g. *radar* (*ra*dio *d*etecting *a*nd *r*anging).

Other acronyms may not make a recognisable word, e.g. *OPEC* (*O*rganisation of *P*etroleum *E*xporting *C*ountries).

ACROSTIC POEM (ack-cros-tick poh-em) A <u>poem</u> written in such a way that the first letter used on each line spells a <u>word</u> which tells what the poem is about.

S	*Sun comes out*
P	*People are happy*
R	*Rain in showers*
I	*In gardens birds sing*
N	*No more winter*
G	*Gardeners are busy*

ACT An act is a major part of a <u>play</u>. It may include several shorter <u>scenes</u>. Often plays are divided into several acts.

ACTIVE VOICE The "voice" of the <u>verb</u> which shows that the <u>subject</u> of the <u>sentence</u> is performing the action.

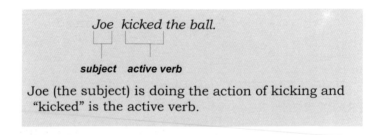

Joe kicked the ball.

subject   active verb

Joe (the subject) is doing the action of kicking and "kicked" is the active verb.

The active "voice" is stronger than the <u>passive voice</u>. The active is used much more often because it is usually shorter and easier to read. (See Verbs – active and passive.)

ACTOR A person who performs a <u>role</u> in a <u>play</u> or <u>drama</u>.

ADAGE (ad-ij) An age-old saying that is short and memorable and which reflects a general truth. An adage gains credit through repeated use.

> *Don't count your chickens before they are hatched.*
>
> means:
> Don't anticipate success, wait until it happens.
>
> *Don't burn your bridges behind you.*
>
> means:
> Don't abandon tried and tested successes as you seek to progress something new, in case you need to rely on them in the future.

ADJECTIVE A describing <u>word</u> that gives more information about <u>nouns</u> or <u>pronouns</u>.

> the *kind* man
>
> the *pretty* flower
>
> it is a *black* cat
>
> she is *happy*

- **simple or ordinary** adjectives are listed in a <u>dictionary</u>, e.g. *rich, kind, pretty.*

- **comparative** adjectives are used when we compare two things or people. We usually add 'r' or 'er' to the simple adjective, e.g. *richer, kinder, prettier.*

- **superlative** adjectives are used when we compare three or more people or things to show which is the most significant. We usually add 'est' to the adjective and put 'the' in front of it, e.g. *the richest, the kindest, the prettiest.*

   (Be careful! Some of the most common adjectives do not follow the normal rules when forming their comparative and superlatives, e.g. *good, better, best.*)

- **interrogative (asking)** adjectives form part of a question.

  > *Which* boy has the ball?
  >
  > *What* coat should I wear?

- **possessive** adjectives show ownership.

  > Patrick always takes *his* golf clubs.
  >
  > Others include *your, their, her, my* and *our.*

- **adjectives of quantity** show the amount of something.

  > He invited *nine* friends on the walk.
  >
  > They did not have *enough* food left.

- **demonstrative** adjectives point things out.

  > *That* girl wore *this* dress.
  >
  > *Those* girls wore *these* dresses.

- **adjectival phrase** is a group of words that does the work of a single adjective.

  > The boy *with brown hair* has just arrived.

- **adjectival clauses** often begin with *whom, that, which, who.*

  > Geoffrey was a person *whom everyone liked.*

ADJUNCT (ad-junkt) A statement in a <u>sentence</u> which, whilst not essential to the structure of the sentence, amplifies its meaning. An adjunct establishes the circumstances in which the action expressed by the verb takes place.

> We waited *for a few moments.*
>
> She will leave *in the afternoon.*
>
> John drank a beer *in the garden.*

An adjunct must always be able to be removed from a sentence and still leave a grammatically well-formed sentence.

An adjunct contrasts with a <u>complement</u> which, when omitted from a sentence, sometimes leaves it grammatically incorrect.

> John is *in the garden.*

ADVERB tells us more about the verb. Adverbs mainly tell us:

- *how* an action is done, e.g. *quickly, slowly, carefully.* These '*how*' adverbs are often formed from <u>adjective</u>s by adding '*ly*'. These are called Adverbs of Manner.

- *when* an action is done, e.g. *now, immediately, yesterday.* These are called Adverbs of Time.

- *where* an action takes place, e.g. *here, there, away.* These are called Adverbs of Place.

- ***adverbial phrases*** – sometimes we use a group of <u>word</u>s, a <u>phrase</u>, instead of one adverb.

> She arrived *early.*   (adverb)
>
>   could become:
>
> She arrived at *exactly ten o'clock.* (adverbial phrase)

- **_comparative_** adverbs are used to compare how actions are performed.

> Steve eats _more_ than Graham.
>
> Christine climbed _higher_ than Amber.
>
> You did _better_ than before.

When adverbs end in 'ly', use 'more' or 'most' before the adverb to make comparisons.

> Steve eats _more quickly_ than Graham.
>
> Of the three people, Dave searched the _most carefully_.

You add 'er' and 'est' to some adverbs to make comparisons.

> He jumped _higher_ than her.
>
> Of the three, he jumped the _highest._

AIDE MÉMOIRE (aid-mem-wah) A memory aid that is used to help remember things, e.g. _notes, lists, diagrams, pictures, mnemonics._

ALLEGORY (all-eh-gor-ee) A <u>story</u> with more than one meaning. Often a simple story will conceal a much deeper <u>tale</u>.

ALLITERATION (al-lit-er-ay-shun) (Also see Rhetorical Device.) This is achieved when particular <u>letters</u> or sounds (usually <u>consonant</u>s) are repeated at the beginning of <u>word</u>s to produce an interesting effect.

> _She sells sea shells on the sea shore._
>
> _Around the rugged rocks the ragged rascal ran._

ALLUSION (al-loo-shun) A <u>literary</u> device that encourages
different ideas and associations to be made using only a
few <u>words</u>. It involves no outright or explicit mention of
the person or thing the writer or speaker has in mind.
Allusion relies on the reader or hearer being able to
understand the allusion and being able to connect with the
meaning hidden behind the words.

> "He's a real *Romeo.*"
>
> > (From the character in '*Romeo and Juliet*' by
> > William Shakespeare. It is suggestive of a person's
> > desire for love and affairs of the heart.)
>
> "You're such a *Scrooge.*"
>
> > (From the character portrayed in '*A Christmas
> > Carol*' by Charles Dickens. It suggests a person is
> > mean and ungenerous, particularly with money.)

ALPHABET (alf-a-bet) Written English uses the Roman
alphabet which has 26 <u>letters</u> altogether. These can be
written as small letters (<u>lower case</u>) or <u>capital letters</u>
(<u>upper case</u>).

> *a b c d e f g h i j k l m n o p q r s t u v w x y z*
>
> *A B C D E F G H I J K L M N O P Q R S T U V W X Y Z*

ALPHABETICAL ORDER (alf-a-bet-ick-al or-der) A <u>dictionary</u>
begins with all the <u>words</u> starting with A. Next follow all
those starting with B, then C and so on through the
<u>alphabet</u>. The definitions in this book are written in
alphabetical order.

   ◆ <u>Words</u> starting with the same letter are sorted by
the alphabetical order of the second letter.

> c<u>a</u>t comes before c<u>r</u>awl
>
> m<u>a</u>n comes before m<u>e</u>n

- Where groups of words start with the same <u>letters</u> they are in order of the next letter of each word.

> wa<u>k</u>e comes before wa<u>l</u>k
>
> batt<u>e</u>r comes before batt<u>l</u>e

- Where two words begin in the same way but one word is shorter than the other, the order in which the words are placed depends on the next letter placed in alphabetical order.

> *cat* comes before *catch*
>
> *catapult* comes after *cat* but before *catch*

- Where words start with the same letters and then in a longer word there are double letters that are the same, the shorter word would come first.

> *cat* comes before *cattle*
>
> *bat* comes before *battle*

AMANUENSIS (uh-man-yoo-en-sis) A person whose job or task it is to write what someone dictates or to copy what has been written by someone else.

AMBIGUITY (am-big-yoo-it-ee) A double meaning or an expression capable of more than one meaning. In <u>writing</u> it exists when a <u>sentence</u> or passage has more than one meaning and the reader has no way of telling which one the writer intended.

"You must speak English."
This could mean,
   it is essential to speak in English.
or it could mean,
   I know that you can speak English therefore you
   should do so.

AMERICANISM Dialect words used in the USA which have slightly different meanings from those commonly used in English.

drapes	⟹	*curtains*
candy	⟹	*sweets*
diapers	⟹	*nappies*

ANAGRAM A word formed from the letters of another word.

The letters in the word *teacher* can become *cheater*

so *cheater* is an anagram of *teacher*

and *teacher* is an anagram of *cheater*

ANALOGY (a-nal-oh-jee) A comparison that can be made between two different things in order to identify a point of similarity. A simile is an expressed analogy. A metaphor is an implied analogy. A parable uses a story to illustrate a comparison.

ANALYSE (an-a-lise) A command word sometimes used in an examination or literacy question. It requires you to break down the topic into the key features and give a structured, in-depth account to make it clear and understandable.

ANALYSIS (an-al-eh-sis) The process of breaking up a <u>sentence</u> into its separate parts to show how those parts are related to one another, e.g. in a <u>simple sentence</u> identifying the <u>subject</u> and <u>predicate</u>.

ANECDOTE (an-eck-dote) A little <u>story</u> told by someone about things that have happened to them. Anecdotes are often funny and are told to make people laugh and/or to make a point.

ANNOTATION (an-no-tay-shun) A written note added to a piece of <u>text</u>, usually in the <u>margin</u>, to give <u>comment</u> on or explanation of a particular section of the text.

ANTAGONIST The main opponent of the principal <u>character</u> in a work of <u>literature</u>. The antagonist is the counterpart to the main character (known as the <u>protagonist</u>). Their interaction provides the source of a <u>story</u>'s main <u>conflict</u>. The antagonist need not necessarily be bad or evil but they will oppose the protagonist in a significant way.

> In the stories of 'Robin Hood and his Merry Men' the Sheriff of Nottingham is the antagonist to Robin Hood (the protagonist).

ANTHOLOGY (an-thol-o-gee) A <u>book</u> or collection of selected <u>writings</u>, usually comprising the most popular and well-liked by one <u>author</u> or <u>poet</u>.

It can also be from the works of different authors or poets, often in the same <u>literary</u> form from the same period or about the same subject.

ANTITHESIS (an-tith-eh-sis) A <u>figure of speech</u> that contrasts ideas using <u>words</u> or <u>sentence</u> associations to convey an exact opposite meaning.

"One small step for man, one giant leap for mankind"
– Neil Armstrong

"Actions not words"

"Not that I loved Caesar less but that I loved Rome more"
– Brutus   from "Julius Caesar", by William Shakespeare

ANTONYM (an-toh-nim) (Also known as an <u>Opposite</u>.) A <u>word</u> that has the opposite meaning to another word.

noisy	⇒	*silent*
good	⇒	*bad*
happy	⇒	*sad*

Antonyms or opposites can sometimes be made by:

- adding a <u>prefix</u>

happy	⇒	*un*happy
lock	⇒	*un*lock
obey	⇒	*dis*obey

- changing the prefix

*in*side	⇒	*out*side
*in*crease	⇒	*de*crease
*en*courage	⇒	*dis*courage

- changing the <u>suffix</u>

care*ful*	⇒	care*less*
use*ful*	⇒	use*less*

APHORISM (a-for-is-um) A term for speech and <u>writing</u> that is short, direct and memorable. Aphorisms often relate to abstract truth rather than to practical matters.

> *"Marry in haste: repent at leisure"*
>
> *"One man's meat is another man's poison"*
>
> *"Lost time is never found again"*   - Benjamin Franklin
>
> *"That which does not destroy us makes us stronger"*   - Friedrich Nietzsche
>
> *"Power corrupts and absolute power corrupts absolutely"*   - Lord Acton

APOSTROPHE (a-pos-tro-fee) A <u>punctuation</u> mark with two uses.

- **in shortened words** – when we speak we often shorten two <u>word</u>s and use them as one. In <u>writing</u>, the apostrophe shows where <u>letters</u> have been missed out.

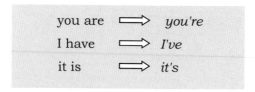

you are	⟹	*you're*
I have	⟹	*I've*
it is	⟹	*it's*

- **to show possession** – an apostrophe can also mean that something belongs to someone or something.

  If there is only one owner, so the word is a <u>singular</u> word, use the apostrophe followed by *s*.

> the *boy's* book
>
> the *cat's* paw

If there is more than one owner, so the word is <u>plural</u> and the word ends in *s* or *es*, add the apostrophe after the *s.*

> the *boys'* bats
>
> the *girls'* games

If there is more than one owner and the plural word does not normally end in an *s*, e.g. *men, children, women*, add the apostrophe and then the *s* to show the owners.

> the *men's* holidays
>
> the *children's* game
>
> the *women's* clothes

Be careful! Some possessive (or belonging words) don't have any apostrophe at all, e.g. *its, hers, ours, theirs, his, yours.* These are known as <u>possessive pronouns</u>.

Sometimes for inanimate objects, it is usually best to use an 'of ' <u>phrase</u> before the object.

> the smell *of* the grease paint
>
> the roar *of* the crowd

However, sometimes an apostrophe of possession can accompany an inanimate object.

> a *year's* salary
>
> my *heart's* desire
>
> your *money's* worth
>
> the *story's* conclusion

APPENDIX A short listing of important facts and details that may be presented as a table. It comes at the end of a book and summarises information about the book.

ARCHAIC LANGUAGE (ar-kay-ick lang-gwi-j) Words or phrases that are no longer in everyday use, e.g. *thou, hither, betwixt, transistor radio.*

Archaic language is still encountered in older literature and is still sometimes used in modern writing to create a special effect.

ARGUMENT (ar-gue-ment) The collection of the reasons and points that are presented in response to a question, issue or task. It sets out and explains the point of view that the writer is taking.

ARTICLE (ar-tick-ul) A piece of writing, often short, giving information on a particular topic or issue, written in a newspaper style with a headline and possibly using subtitles too.

ARTICLES (ar-tick-uls) Three little words, *'the'* (definite article), *'a'* and *'an'* (indefinite article).

ARTISTIC LICENCE (art-iss-tick li-sense) When an author makes changes for the sake of the story. Maybe an historical fact is altered, or places are moved to suit the needs of the plot. (Also known as Dramatic Licence.)

ASIDE In a play, a speech delivered in a way that other characters cannot hear but the audience can. This provides the audience with extra information which may inform their overall understanding of the play. (Also see Soliloquy.)

ASSONANCE (ass-o-nanse) A poetic device, using a sound pattern, where the vowel sounds are repeated to give a rhyming effect.

How now brown cow?

The fat cat sat on the mat.

ASTERISK A star (*) shaped <u>punctuation</u> mark used to show the reader something important in the <u>text</u>. They can be used in place of <u>bullet point</u>s at the start of a new point to identify it and also inside the text to draw the reader's attention to a <u>footnote</u>.

ATMOSPHERE (at-moss-fear) A particular feeling or influence or <u>mood</u>, created by a <u>play</u>, <u>book</u>, film or event, e.g. *There was an atmosphere of excitement* or *there was an atmosphere of mystery.*

AUDIENCE (ord-ee-ence) The people whom a writer is expecting to read his or her <u>book</u>. They are also the people who would be watching a <u>play</u> or <u>pantomime</u> or listening to a radio programme.

AUTHOR (or-ther) The real person who wrote the <u>text</u> of a <u>novel</u> or <u>story</u>.

AUTOBIOGRAPHY (or-toh-bi-og-ra-fee) The true <u>story</u> about one's own life written by yourself.

BACKSTORY In <u>narrative</u> <u>literature</u>, this is the history that exists for the <u>character</u>s and other features of the <u>story</u> at the point where the main story begins. A backstory helps to set the main story in a <u>context</u> and it may be revealed in parts or in full as the main narrative unfolds.

In journalism, the backstory is different and for the news <u>media</u> it is generally considered to be any information that does not make it into the story as reported. This may be because the subject is too diverse and complicated, or it may be because it does not meet <u>editorial</u> or journalistic standards. Such backstories may be based on information from secret sources, unconfirmed rumour or evidence that may not be totally reliable.

BALLAD (bal-uhd) A <u>poem</u> or <u>song</u> that tells a <u>story</u> – often an adventure or love story. Ballads are usually long and have many <u>verses</u>. Most ballads follow a <u>rhyme scheme</u>.

BIAS (bi-uhs) The way in which a <u>text</u> communicates information based on selecting and presenting facts and details in a way that represents the truth but which is influenced by a variety of values, attitudes and opinions. The aim of bias is to persuade, change opinions and affect final outcomes.

BIBLIOGRAPHY (bib-lee-og-ra-fee) The history, listing, classification or description of <u>books</u> including details of <u>author</u>, <u>editor</u>, publisher and date of publication.

BIOGRAPHY (bi-og-ra-fee) The life <u>story</u> of a real person, not written by themselves, but written by somebody else.

BLANK VERSE has a <u>metre</u> but does not <u>rhyme</u>. Blank verse usually has lines containing ten <u>syllables</u>, five of them stressed and five unstressed. Many of William Shakespeare's <u>plays</u> contain blank verse which is often employed to denote a <u>character</u>'s status or importance.

BLURB appears on the back of a <u>book</u> and gives the main outline or <u>synopsis</u> of the <u>story</u> so you know what the book is about. It won't reveal the ending and is written in such a way as to persuade you to want to read the book.

BOOK A printed or written work comprising sheets of paper bound together. A book may have a protective cover and is usually considered to provide a source of knowledge, education or entertainment.

A book can be a part of a collection of books that put together comprise a major <u>literary</u> work, e.g. *The Holy Bible is a collection of 66 books written by different authors.*

BOOK REVIEW A written account which gives an evaluation of a <u>book</u> from the perspective of one who has read it. A review covers:

- basic information, e.g. *title, author, publisher* and *illustrator* (if any)
- summary of the <u>story</u>
- <u>genre</u>, e.g. *mystery, detective, science fiction, etc.*
- <u>setting</u>, e.g. *where the story takes place*
- <u>plot</u>, e.g. *fast-paced, confusing, easy to follow, etc.*
- <u>characters</u>
- <u>author</u>'s choice of <u>language</u>
- the reviewer's opinion

BRACKETS are punctuation marks and are used in pairs and enclose information offering further explanation of the main thrust of a sentence.

- ◆ There are occasions when either <u>commas</u> or brackets could be correctly used: it is up to the writer. Generally brackets are used when you want to keep the enclosed information rather more hidden away.

> Arrive promptly at the house (remembering to use the correct password), bring all the equipment and especially the food.

- ◆ When there are brackets in the same place as a <u>punctuation</u> mark that would normally belong to the main <u>sentence</u>, put the punctuation mark after the second bracket.

> Arrive promptly at the house (remembering to use the correct password)**,** bring all the equipment and especially the food.

- If the complete sentence is written inside brackets you need to begin it with a <u>capital letter</u> and end it with a <u>full stop</u> which is placed inside the brackets.

> Arrive promptly at the house. (Make sure you remember to use the correct password.) Bring all the equipment and especially the food.

- If the words in brackets come at the end of a sentence, put the full stop after the second bracket.

> Make sure you bring all the food (chocolate, crisps, cakes and sandwiches).

Sometimes the words within brackets can be said to be "in <u>parentheses</u>".

BRAINSTORM (See Mind-Mapping and Thought Shower.)

BROADSHEET WRITING (Also see Newspaper.) A <u>style of writing</u> used in some <u>newspapers</u> that sets out to report news in a serious <u>tone</u>. It is characterised by:

- factual and informative reporting of news

- opinion columns separated from news items

- longer and more detailed news <u>report</u>s

- <u>language</u> levels that are more demanding to read

- separate sections giving information and reports, e.g. *Travel, Finance, Sport, Books and the Arts*

Examples of broadsheet style <u>writing</u> are found in The Times, The Guardian and The Daily Telegraph newspapers.

BULLET POINTS Usually dots (•) but sometimes other shapes, used in <u>writing</u> to help the reader identify new points being made by the writer. Bullet points are used at the beginning of each new <u>paragraph</u> to show where the new point begins, e.g. see the bullet points used above in the <u>definition</u> of <u>Broadsheet Writing</u>.

Bullet points are not usually acceptable in formal writing styles such as essays but they can be used effectively in reports, leaflets and posters.

BUZZWORD An idiom, often with an unclear meaning. The use of such words is recognised widely and they are frequently used to impress an audience with the pretence of knowledge. They make sentences difficult to dispute on account of their imprecise meaning, e.g. *globalisation, empowerment, framework, next generation, proactive, downsizing.*

CALLIGRAM (cal-ee-gram) A poem that is written using distinctive letter shapes and thickness to represent what the poem is about.

thin, spiky letters	⟹	horror
fat, blobby letters	⟹	food
twig shapes	⟹	trees

CAPITAL LETTER is used at the beginning of:

- sentences, e.g. *We went home.*
- people's names, e.g. *John, Don, Katie*
- Holy names, e.g. *Jesus, God, Allah, Buddha*
- names of places, e.g. *Britain, Yorkshire, West Ham*
- months, days of week and special days, e.g. *November, Monday, Christmas*
- the words in the titles of books, plays, songs, newspapers, films and poems, e.g. *The Daily Sun, The Incredibles*
- company names and products, e.g. *After Eight Mints, Waitrose*
- important building names, e.g. *Buckingham Palace*
- rivers, mountains and sea, e.g. *River Thames*

- adjectives derived from the names of countries, e.g. *French, Swiss*

- names of streets and roads, e.g. *Station Road*

- each new line in a poem

and for:

- some abbreviations, e.g. *BBC, ITV*

- the personal pronoun "I", e.g. *I went to bed.*

CAPTION (cap-shun) A phrase beneath a picture, photograph or cartoon that helps the viewer understand what the picture is about.

CARICATURE (carr-i-ca-ture) In literature, a description of a person using exaggeration of some distinctive features, peculiarities or characteristics and oversimplification of others. Caricatures can be insulting or complimentary and may be used as a feature of satire or lampoon.

CATCHLINE (See Strapline. Also known as a Tagline.)

CATCHPHRASE (catch fray-se) A phrase or expression that is widely recognised due to its repeated usage. Comedians and politicians often become closely associated with phrases they have made popular.

> *"Tough on crime, tough on the causes of crime."*
>
> *"Education, education, education."*
>
>   - Tony Blair, former British Prime Minister
>
> *"Nice to see you, to see you, nice."*
>
>   - Bruce Forsyth, British comedian

CATCHWORD A favourite, memorable or effective word or phrase that is repeated so often that it becomes a slogan. Such words can be made popular by a political or advertising campaign.

- Also a word printed at the top of a page in a dictionary to indicate the first or last entry on that page. (See Index Words.)

- Among theatrical performers, the last word or cue word of the preceding speaker which reminds the next actor that they are next to speak.

CHAPTER A section in a novel that tells you part of the story. It breaks the story up to show that time has passed, or to tell the reader about a different place or to introduce new characters.

CHARACTER (kar-act-er) A person who is portrayed in a book, film or play.

CHARACTER SKETCH (kar-act-er ske-tch) A brief narrative that describes and reveals a character's traits or personality.

CHARADE (shu-rahd) A word, number of words, phrase or title which is acted out in a game of charades.

CHARADES (shu-rahds) A game in which words or phrases are represented in a mimed drama or play sometimes syllable by syllable. The game involves at least two teams, members of which act out the word that the members of their own team must guess.

CHORUS (cor-us) Found in songs and poems as a group of lines that are repeated between the verses. The words found in the chorus are always the same.

In plays by William Shakespeare, the Chorus is a kind of story teller. The Chorus can be a man or a woman and their speeches are there to set the scene. They inform where the action is and describe the scene for the audience especially if it is something that cannot be shown properly on stage. The Chorus encourages the audience members to use their imaginations using plenty of poetic descriptions to help them.

CINQUAIN (sin-kwan) A <u>poem</u> which has five lines that do not <u>rhyme</u>. They follow a particular pattern of <u>syllables</u> which goes:

Line No	No. of syllables
1	2
2	4
3	6
4	8
5	2

Each poem has twenty-two <u>syllables</u> altogether.

	syllables
Winter	2
Skies are so grey	4
We all must stay indoors	6
Christmas always brings us bright hope	8
Of peace	2

CLAUSE (clors) A group of <u>words</u> containing a <u>subject</u> and a <u>verb</u>. It is not a <u>sentence</u> as it does not need a <u>capital letter</u> or a <u>full stop</u>.

- a *simple* one clause sentence is always made up of two parts:-

  ◆ a subject (who or what the sentence is about)

  ◆ a <u>predicate </u>(the rest of the sentence)

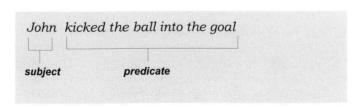

- **a main (independent)** clause is part of a <u>complex sentence</u> which can be used on its own as a sentence as it makes complete sense

- **subordinate (dependent)** clauses are less important clauses in a complex sentence which do not make sense on their own

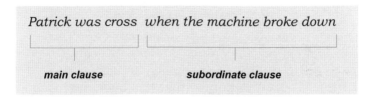

Moving the position of a subordinate clause is good for building sentence variety.

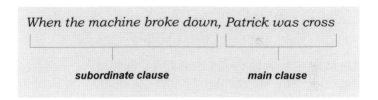

- **a drop-in** clause is a clause separated by <u>commas</u> that can be dropped into a <u>simple sentence</u>

> *Dave is young and handsome*

can become:

> *Dave, known as the Tutor Master, is young and handsome*

- **relative** clauses use 'who' or 'which'

> *Don, who lives in Windsor, is a Swindon supporter.*
>
> *The advice, which I got from Mary, really helped me with my story writing.*

CLERIHEW (cle-ree-huw) A humorous <u>poem</u> of four lines set out in two <u>rhyming couplets</u>. They say something funny about a person whose name forms the first line of the poem.

> *Sir Donald Ross*
>
> *Said, "I'm feeling quite cross."*
>
> *My team lose every game*
>
> *It seems such a shame!*

CLICHÉ (clee-shay) A <u>phrase</u> that has been overused in everyday speech so that it no longer sounds original and its impact has been lost.

> *At the end of the day* we all need to see *the light at the end of the tunnel.*

CLIFFHANGER A technique used by writers to make a <u>story</u> exciting. The story might finish suddenly and probably unexpectedly or the story may be interrupted. The reader is left to work out for themselves the likely outcome.

Often a cliffhanger is found at the end of a <u>chapter</u> or story. In this way the writer encourages the reader to continue reading to find out what happens next.

CLIMAX (cly-max) A part of a <u>story structure</u> that follows the <u>crisis</u>. It provides the turning point in a work of <u>literature</u> at which the end result becomes inevitable. The action builds to the climax, which is the high point of the <u>story</u>.

> In '*Romeo and Juliet*' by William Shakespeare, the story reaches its climax in Act 3 when Mercutio and Tybalt are killed and Romeo is banished from Verona.

COHESION (co-hee-shun) The technique of ensuring a <u>text</u> works as a whole. The aim is to link ideas in a flowing way using cohesive devices like <u>phrases</u> or <u>words</u> to help a text develop logically, creating a unified piece.

COLLECTIVE NOUNS (See Noun.)

COLLOQUIALISM (coll-o-kwi-al-ism) An expression used in common conversation.

a chip off the old block ⟹ very like their father
at a loose end ⟹ having nothing to do
good for nothing ⟹ useless

COLON (co-lon) A <u>punctuation mark</u> (:) usually used before a <u>quotation</u>, a contrast of ideas, or to show that something is to follow, which is usually a list but could be an illustration or an explanation. A colon is a stronger punctuation mark than a <u>comma</u> but weaker than a <u>full stop</u>.

COMEDIES (com-med-ees) <u>Plays</u> where the endings are happy and where people may get married, e.g. *'Twelfth Night'* and *'A Midsummer Nights Dream'* by William Shakespeare.

COMMA (commer) A <u>punctuation mark</u> (,) representing the shortest pause in a <u>sentence</u>. It is used to make a much shorter pause than a <u>full stop</u>. A comma is a weaker punctuation mark than a <u>semi-colon</u>.

- ◆ A comma is placed between items in a list to save you repeating the <u>words</u> 'and' or 'or'.

- ◆ A term of address (using a person's name) is always separated from the rest of the sentence with a comma.

> Good morning, Mr Ross.

- ◆ A comma is also used after initial <u>words</u> in sentences.

> Yes, I agree.
>
> Therefore, we will all ...

♦ Pairs of commas are used between words or groups of words which need to be marked off from the rest of the sentence as they are not essential to the meaning. (See Clause.)

> Paul, while climbing the tree, got stuck on a branch.

♦ When a sentence begins with a <u>conjunction</u> (such as 'with', 'when', 'after', 'before', 'until', 'while', 'since', 'if', 'unless', 'although', 'though' or 'because'), as a general rule a comma is used after the group of words that follow the conjunction.

> *If* you buy me these boots, I will play in the match.

♦ A comma follows a <u>subordinate clause</u> when it starts a sentence.

♦ A comma is used to separate <u>direct speech</u> from the rest of the sentence.

COMMA SPLICING (com-mer sply-sing) A common error in <u>writing</u> when a <u>comma</u> is used instead of the correct <u>full stop</u>.

> *I went out early this evening, I didn't have time for dinner.*
>
> A coordinator is needed to connect the two clauses using a full stop, semi-colon or a connective.
>
> *I went out early this evening. I didn't have time for dinner.*
>
> *I went out early this evening; I didn't have time for dinner.*
>
> *I went out early this evening, and I didn't have time for dinner.*

COMMAND SENTENCE (Also known as an Imperative.) Gives an order or a request.

> *Do not run in the corridor.*

COMMAND WORD A <u>word</u> used by examiners in a <u>question</u> that instructs you to write a particular kind of response, e.g. *<u>analyse</u>, <u>comment</u>, <u>compare</u>, <u>contrast</u>, <u>describe</u>, <u>discuss</u>, <u>evaluate</u>, <u>examine</u>, <u>explain</u>, <u>explore</u>, <u>investigate</u>, <u>suggest</u>,* etc.

> *Compare* the ways Walton and Roberts react to their situations in lines 17 to 61. *Comment* on the language the writer uses to convey their reactions.

COMMENT A <u>command word</u> sometimes used in an examination or <u>literacy question</u>. This means you have to consider all the information that you have that is relevant to the question. You should identify and summarise the main points and then give your opinion as to their significance, supported by evidence.

COMMENTARY A <u>comment</u> or observation, which may be spoken or written, about a piece of <u>writing</u> or an event. A written commentary may be placed alongside a difficult <u>text</u> explaining what it is about, what the harder <u>word</u>s mean and providing an explanation of the <u>imagery</u>.

A spoken commentary (also known as a running commentary) gives a series of comments provided by an observer of an event such as a cricket or football match, or a horse race. (Also see Continuous Tense.)

COMMON NOUN (See Noun.)

COMPARATIVE (See Adjective.)

COMPARE A command word sometimes used in an examination or literacy question which means you are to examine two or more ideas, views or aims, etc. in order to note similarities and differences. A concluding written statement should summarise the points identified during the process of comparing.

COMPENDIUM (com-pen-dih-um) A concise, brief but comprehensive summary of a larger work or area of human interest.

> An encyclopaedia can be referred to as a *"compendium of all human knowledge"*.
>
> The Oxford English Dictionary sets out to provide a *"compendium (comprehensive compilation) of words in the English language"*.

COMPLEMENT (kom-pluh-muhnt) Some verbs require some other part of speech to make the sense complete, e.g. If we say 'Sir Francis Drake was ...', we feel something is missing. If we add 'a navigator and sailor' the sense is complete and we have a sentence. The words that were added to complete the sentence are called the complement.

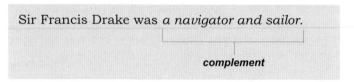

Sir Francis Drake was *a navigator and sailor.*

complement

COMPLEX SENTENCE Contains one main clause which can be used on its own as a sentence and one or more subordinate (less important) clauses which do not make sense on their own.

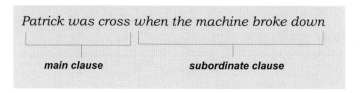

Patrick was cross when the machine broke down

main clause   *subordinate clause*

COMPLICATION (comp-lih-kay-shun) The part of a <u>story structure</u> that sets out the events that follow the <u>exposition</u> and which introduces the <u>conflict</u>.

COMPREHENSION (comp-re-hen-shun) The range of skills developed by reading and understanding the written <u>word</u>. This may be understanding information from <u>fiction</u>, <u>non-fiction</u>, <u>poems</u>, tables and charts. Skills developed could be:

- ◆ literal comprehension (understanding exactly what is in the <u>text</u>)
- ◆ collecting and re-organising information
- ◆ recall (remembering what has been read)
- ◆ evaluation, appreciation and opinion
- ◆ making deductions, e.g. *what may happen next*
- ◆ making inferences, e.g. *what if this were to happen*

COMPOUND PRONOUN (Also known as a Reflexive Pronoun.)

COMPOSITION (komp-oh-sish-shun) The act of putting together <u>word</u>s into <u>sentence</u>s and putting these together to produce a piece of <u>literature</u>.

COMPOUND SENTENCE (kom-pound sent-en-se) A <u>sentence</u> made up of two or more short sentences joined by a <u>conjunction</u> or separated by a <u>comma</u>, <u>semi-colon</u> or <u>colon</u>. Compound sentences are a good way to add variety to <u>writing</u> and make it flow better, but should not be used too frequently.

> The footballer took a shot. The ball hit the post.
>
> *The footballer took a shot <u>but</u> the ball hit the post.*
>
> ⬆
>
> ***conjunction***

COMPOUND WORD (kom-pound word) comprises two or more words joined together.

- Two words joined together, e.g. *bedroom, fireman, lighthouse*

- Two words joined with a hyphen, e.g. *high-class, self-service, dry-clean*

- Two separate words used together as one noun, e.g. *living room, tape measure, ice cream*

CONCLUSION (con-klu-shun) The final part of an essay, composition, report or letter. A conclusion is necessary where a piece of writing has addressed a question, hypothesis or issue. The purpose of the conclusion is to give an answer, final statement or response to the question after having considered the relevant evidence, facts or information.

CONCRETE NOUN (con-creet nown) (See Noun.)

CONCRETE POEM (con-creet po-em) (Also known as a Shape Poem.) A poem that involves drawing a picture or shape to accompany the poem. The words are written as a part of the drawing or shape to help illustrate what the poem is about.

CONDITIONAL TENSE (con-di-shun-al ten-se) An action that is conditional on something else. It may take place if something else happens first.

> I *would play* if I had a pair of boots.
>
> You *would go* if you had the day off.

CONFLICT (con-flikt) The part of a <u>story structure</u> which follows the <u>complication</u>. It features the struggle between opposing forces which provides the main action in a piece of <u>literature</u>. The desire to find out how the <u>story</u> resolves the conflict is what makes a reader keep reading.

Conflicts can be identified in many forms such as:

♦ between individual <u>characters</u>, e.g. *Prince Caspian and King Miraz* in the book 'Prince Caspian' by C.S. Lewis

♦ between groups of characters, e.g. *the Montague and Capulets* in the <u>play</u> 'Romeo and Juliet' by William Shakespeare

♦ between individual characters and nature, e.g. *Robinson Crusoe* in the book 'Robinson Crusoe' by Daniel Defoe

♦ between individuals and society, e.g. *Winston Smith and The Party* in the book '1984' by George Orwell

CONJUGATION (con-ju-gay-shun) A way of showing how a verb can be arranged in order to show all its parts. English <u>verbs</u> may form their <u>past</u> <u>tense</u> and <u>past participle</u> by adding 'd', 'ed' or 't' to the <u>present tense.</u>

The following two charts show the conjugation of the verb *'to walk'* in all its parts. The <u>word</u>s in <u>italics</u> show the <u>continuous tense</u> of the <u>word</u> to show that the action is going on for some time.

The traditional distinction between using 'shall' and 'will' is generally considered to be no longer important and in common English usage either can be used correctly.

Verb Tense Chart

Subject	Present (Simple)	Past (Simple)	Future (Simple)
I [1st person]	walk *am walking*	walked *was walking*	shall walk *shall be walking*
You (singular) [2nd person]	walk *are walking*	walked *were walking*	will walk *will be walking*
he/she/it [3rd person]	walks *is walking*	walked *was walking*	will walk *will be walking*
We (plural) [1st person]	walk *are walking*	walked *were walking*	shall walk *shall be walking*
You (plural) [2nd person]	walk *are walking*	walked *were walking*	will walk *will be walking*
They (plural) [3rd person]	walk *are walking*	walked *were walking*	will walk *will be walking*

Verb Tense Chart

Subject	Present Perfect	Past Perfect	Future Perfect
I [1st person]	have walked *have been walking*	had walked *had been walking*	shall have walked *shall have been walking*
You (singular) [2nd person]	have walked *have been walking*	had walked *had been walking*	will have walked *will have been walking*
he/she/it [3rd person]	has walked *has been walking*	had walked *had been walking*	will have walked *will have been walking*
We (plural) [1st person]	have walked *have been walking*	had walked *had been walking*	shall have walked *shall have been walking*
You (plural) [2nd person]	have walked *have been walking*	had walked *had been walking*	will have walked *will have been walking*
They (plural) [3rd person]	have walked *have been walking*	had walked *had been walking*	will have walked *will have been walking*

CONJUNCTION (con-junk-shun) (Also known as Connective and a Linking Word.) is a joining <u>word</u>. Conjunctions are used to join other words and parts of <u>sentences</u> together. In <u>writing</u> they are useful to make sentences longer.

> The footballer took a shot. The ball hit the post.
>
> *The footballer took a shot <u>but</u> the ball hit the post.*
>
> ⬆
>
> *conjunction*

Time conjunctions are used to join sentences and parts of sentences using time related words.

> *after, when, before, since, until, whenever.*

CONNECTIVE (See Conjunction.)

CONSONANT Each letter of the <u>alphabet</u> which is **not** a <u>vowel</u> (a, e, i, o, u). All the other <u>letters</u> are consonants.

> *b c d f g h j k l m n p q r s t v w x y z*

CONTENT What is included within a <u>text</u>. It is what the text is about.

CONTENTS The list found at the start of a <u>book</u> or <u>magazine</u> which tells you what is in the book and the page number where something can be found.

CONTEXT The background to a particular <u>text</u>, e.g. when and where it was written. These factors influence the <u>text</u>. The historical, social and <u>literacy</u> context of a text is often worth exploring.

CONTINUOUS TENSE (con-tin-you-us ten-se) (Also see Conjugation.) Shows that the action is going on for some time.

	using continuous tense
I chase.	_I am chasing._
I chased.	_I was chasing._
I shall chase.	_I shall be chasing._

If something is happening continuously, the continuous tense is much more useful. It is used in radio and TV commentaries when an event is being broadcast live.

> _I am standing at the match. The players are already out. Sadly, it is raining ..._

CONTRACTION (con-track-shun) is a shortened word. The original long word is hardly used at all.

> We say:
>
> _plane_ instead of _aeroplane_
>
> _photo_ instead of _photograph_
>
> _phone_ instead of _telephone_

Contractions can also be the shortened form of two words by use of an apostrophe.

> _we're_ instead of _we are_
>
> _shan't_ instead of _shall not_

CONTRAST A command word sometimes used in an examination or literacy question. It means you have to compare things and distinguish between them by showing or emphasising the differences between them. A concluding written statement will set out the main differences identified.

CONUNDRUM A term for a riddle, difficult problem or question based upon an unusual resemblance between things quite unlike. A puzzling question which in itself may be a pun or a play on words or where the answer is (or involves) a pun.

What is black and white and read [red] all over?
[Answer: A newspaper]

If fire fighters fight fires and crime fighters fight crime, what do freedom fighters fight?

If you try to fail, but you succeed, which have you done?

When is a door not a door?
[Answer: When it's ajar (a jar)]

What's brown and sticky?
[Answer: A stick]

Why is six afraid of seven?
[Answer: Because seven ate (eight) nine]

COUPLET (cup-let) (See Rhyming Couplet.)

CRISIS (cry-sis) The part of the story structure that follows the rising action and which provides a decisive moment for the protagonist and their commitment to a cause of action.

CRITICISM (crit-ih-sis-um) Writing or speech which comments on and gives an opinion about what someone else has written, said or done. Criticism analyses, judges or interprets the works of writers, artists, scientists, musicians or actors. It is based on individual opinion and viewpoint.

CURRICULUM VITAE (curr-ick-u-lum vee-tay) A Latin term meaning 'what you've done in your life'. A written account in list format detailing factual information about a person's life history. The audience for a CV is usually a prospective employer so it details qualifications, experience and jobs plus personal details such as date of birth and contact details.

CURSIVE (ker-siv) Handwriting characterised by a flowing style with the <u>letters</u> joined together. It is also the style of a letter or character set on typeface that appears like handwriting.

Peter and Valerie have beautiful cursive handwriting.

DANGLING MODIFIER When a <u>word</u> or <u>phrase</u> causes confusion because in the <u>sentence</u> it is located too far away from the word to which it refers.

I saw a shark snorkelling.
(Whilst snorkelling I saw a shark.)

"The other day I shot an elephant in my pyjamas – How he got in my pyjamas I'll never know" Groucho Marks.
(The other day, whilst in my pyjamas, I shot an elephant.)

I bought the chair from the shopkeeper with the padded bottom.
(I bought the chair with the padded bottom from the shopkeeper.)

DASHES <u>Punctuation marks</u> (-) that are generally used in pairs. Their use is to enclose information which is not part of the main meaning of the <u>sentence</u>. Dashes are used mainly to give a slight sense of impact and do not hide the information quite so much as <u>brackets</u>.

Generally brackets mark the strongest division and dashes mark a less strong division between <u>words</u> in <u>parentheses</u> and the rest of the sentence.

The referee – glancing at his watch – blew his whistle.

As soon as it was dark – which was early as it was winter – they set off.

- Dashes can also be used singly to mark a pause in a sentence to give a dramatic effect.

> I searched high and low and suddenly there it was – the missing pen.

- Dashes can be used to separate a list from its summary.

> The case contains – pencils, pens, rubbers.
>
> Radishes, turnips, swedes, carrots – my favourite root vegetables.

DEBATE A discussion between two people or two groups of people who have conflicting opinions and views on an issue. A debate focuses on a statement which is proposed by one side and opposed by the other. After the debate a vote is taken by the <u>audience</u> to establish which set of views was more convincing.

DEFINITE ARTICLE (def-in-ate ar-tick-al) The <u>word</u> 'the' used in a <u>sentence</u> to identify or specify a particular thing.

DEFINITION (def-in-i-shun) The written meaning of a <u>word</u> or <u>phrase</u>.

DEMONSTRATIVE PRONOUN (See Pronoun.)

DENOUEMENT (dey-noo-mahn) A French <u>word</u> meaning "the action of untying". (See Resolution.)

DEPENDENT CLAUSE (Also known as a Subordinate Clause. See Clause.)

DESCRIBE (de-scry-be) A <u>command word</u> sometimes used in an examination or <u>literacy question</u> when the examiner or teacher wants you to explain or give a careful account of the facts, details or particulars of something. N.B. Unless the question asks you both to *describe* and *explain*, just write the description and avoid using the <u>word</u> 'because.'

DEVICE (de-vi-se) (See Poetic Device.)

DIALECT (di-al-ect) <u>Words</u> or <u>phrases</u> which are familiar to and used by people living in a particular region of a country. People from outside the region may have difficulty understanding the meaning of dialect words and phrases.

DIALOGUE (di-a-log) Any part of <u>text</u> where the <u>characters</u> speak. Dialogue is set out in the text using the rules for punctuating <u>direct speech</u>. Dialogue is used to make characters sound life-like, to list what the characters are saying to one another and to help the reader to know more about them.

DIARY (di-a-ree) A daily record written by one person which records their thoughts, feelings, observations and experiences. Diaries are private <u>books</u> usually read only by the <u>author</u>. Diaries are often written in the style of the <u>first person</u>, <u>narrative voice</u> using "I" and "me".

DICTION (dick-shun) is concerned with the <u>style of writing</u> and the <u>author</u>'s choice of <u>words</u>. It takes into account correctness, arrangements, clarity, effectiveness and the force, accuracy and distinction with which words are used.

Diction is also concerned with the style of speaking relating to <u>pronunciation</u>, particularly the <u>accent</u>, <u>inflection</u>, <u>intonation</u> and speech-sound quality exhibited by an individual speaker, e.g. *The speaker was distinguished by his excellent diction.*

DICTIONARY (dick-shun-airy) A <u>book</u> which lists <u>word</u>s in <u>alphabetical order</u> and tells you what the words mean. It is a collection or <u>compendium</u> of <u>definition</u>s.

DIMINUTIVE (dih-min-u-tiv-e) A <u>word</u> that makes things sound smaller.

kitten	⟹	*kitty*
Tim	⟹	*Timmy*
pig	⟹	*piglet*

A <u>suffix</u> can be added to do this like "kin", "let", or "y" or another word put before it like "tiny", e.g. *Tiny* Tim.

DIRECTOR The person who directs a <u>play</u> or a film. Directors tell the <u>actor</u>s what to do and how to speak in the best way to help the <u>audience</u> understand the production.

DIRECT QUESTION is when the word or words used in the <u>sentence</u> actually form a <u>question</u>. This kind of question expects an answer and has a <u>question mark</u>.

How many goals were scored?

How are you?

What is the date?

DIRECT SPEECH In written work, these are the exact <u>word</u>s spoken by someone. They are always enclosed in <u>speech</u> <u>marks</u>.

- ◆ Always begin speech with a capital letter.

"I've got too much homework today."

- ◆ Enclose the actual words that are spoken within speech marks.

Geoff said, *"I've got too much homework today."*

◆ Separate the words that are actually spoken from the other words with a <u>comma</u>.

> Geoff said, *"I've got too much homework today."*

◆ Make sure <u>question mark</u>s and <u>exclamation mark</u>s are enclosed within the speech marks.

> *"Why are you always complaining about homework?"* asked Anne.

◆ When <u>writing</u> speech conversation or <u>dialogue</u>, make sure you write a new speaker on a new line as a new paragraph.

> *"I'm not always complaining about homework,"* replied Geoff.
>
> *"Oh yes you are!"* shouted Anne.

DISCUSS A <u>command word</u> used in an examination or <u>literacy question</u>. This means you are to give a reasoned response that shows the ability to identify, consider and summarise the points for and against an issue or subject, giving evidence and supported by examples. The process of discussion creates a written <u>debate</u> considering both positive and negative points. A concluding evaluative statement should summarise the outcomes of the discussion.

DISSERTATION (dis-er-tay-shun) A written academic assignment which has been researched and demonstrates a student's <u>writing</u> skills. It is completed by students as a requirement for obtaining a degree, usually of a higher nature such as a doctorate, at a university.

DOCUMENT A written or printed paper with legal or official status which contains information or evidence of a factual nature. It is also a computer data file.

DOCUMENTARY A film, television or radio programme about a real life issue or topic. Documentaries investigate and report facts, information and opinions about the topic or issue and aim to inform the watcher or listener. They tend to be serious in <u>tone</u> in the way they are presented to the <u>audience</u>.

DOUBLES Pairs of <u>words</u> that sound good when put together.

better and *better*	– *repetition of the word*
slip and *slide*	– *alliterative doubles*
in and *out*	– *opposite doubles*
rough and *tumble*	– *repetition of meaning*
fair and *square*	– *rhyming doubles*

DOUBLE NEGATIVE (Also see Litotes.) A grammatical mistake made when two negatives (<u>words</u> meaning "no" or "not") are used in one <u>sentence</u>. They cancel each other out and the negative meaning is lost, just like two negatives in maths.

"I haven't done nothing"
which actually means they have done something!

"We never saw no food for two days"
so they did see some food then!

"The dogs haven't had no biscuits for three days"
so the dogs have had some biscuits!

DRAFT A piece of written work that is often unedited and not the final completed piece. Writers may produce several drafts of a work before they are happy with the final draft. (See Editing.) Usually a draft is preceded by a <u>plan</u>.

DRAMA (drah-mer) This can mean <u>literature</u> written to be performed, or a strong element in <u>writing</u> which creates tension, intrigue or upset.

DRAMATIC IRONY (dram-at-ic i-ron-ee) When the <u>word</u>s and actions of a character in a <u>play</u>, <u>poem</u> or <u>story</u> have a different meaning for the <u>audience</u> because of information already known to the audience.

> *Dave arrives on stage saying, "I can't wait to eat that delicious bowl of strawberries."*
>
> *However, just before his entrance Christine has eaten all the strawberries herself!*
>
> *In Macbeth by William Shakespeare, Macbeth plans the murder of Duncan whilst pretending to be loyal. Duncan does not know of Macbeth's plan but the audience does.*

DRAMATIC LICENCE (dram-at-ic li-sense) (See Artistic Licence.)

DRAMATIC MONOLOGUE (dram-at-ic mon-o-log) A speech made by a character to an imaginary <u>audience</u>, usually at a critical point in the <u>story/play</u> in which the reader gains insight into the character's personality, feelings or motives.

DRAMATIC STRUCTURE (dram-at-ic struck-chur) The elements or parts into which a <u>script</u> or <u>story</u> is divided. These are composed with the aim of capturing the attention of the <u>audience</u> and keeping it. (Also see Story Structure.)

ECHO (ec-ko) A <u>poetic device</u> that repeats a key <u>word</u>, idea, sound or <u>syllable</u> for greater effect.

ECHO VERSE (ec-ko ver-se) A form of <u>poem</u> in which a <u>word</u> or two at the end of a line is repeated with a different <u>spelling</u> or meaning as if in an <u>echo</u>. It may be only one word that makes up the entire following line.

Usually the echo will be <u>indent</u>ed to a point under or below the word it mimics. The last word should be echoed either by <u>repetition</u>, contrast, sound or <u>homophone</u>. The echo can change the meaning in a flippant, cynical or <u>pun</u>ning response.

> I took your poem like a tonic
> Chronic
> Your thoughts were hard to follow
> Swallow
> It was indeed a bitter pill
> Ill
> Although I did my best
> Digest
> Not very much remains
> Pains
> Irony is a form of wit
> Quit!

EDITING Reading back through a draft of written work to correct mistakes in spelling, grammar (especially verb tenses), punctuation and to check that the style of writing is correct for the intended audience.

EDITOR The person responsible for editing.

EDITORIAL (ed-it-or-ee-al) A piece of writing found in a newspaper where comments are written with reference to a piece of current news. The opinions are usually those of the newspaper editor and may contain few actual facts.

E.G. The initial letters for the Latin word exempli gratia meaning 'for example' usually written in lower case: e.g.

ELEGY (el-eh-jee) A form of poetry that mourns the loss of someone who has died or something that has been lost or deteriorated.

> 'Elegy Written in a Country Churchyard'
> by Thomas Gray 1750

ELLIPSIS (...) <u>Full stop</u>s that are used in a row of three to show where a <u>word</u> or <u>phrase</u> has been deliberately left out.

> *Twinkle, twinkle little star how I wonder what you are . . . like a diamond in the sky.*
> (The ellipsis show that the line *"Up above the world so high"* has been left out.)
>
> *Do you always need to finish a sentence?*
> *No, you don't always ...*

A pause, an unfinished thought or a suggestion at the end of a <u>paragraph</u> or <u>sentence</u> that there is more to come, e.g. suspense or a <u>cliffhanger</u> ending.

> *The door creaked, he heard footsteps on the stairs . . .*

EMOTIVE LANGUAGE (e-moh-tiv lang-gwi-dge) <u>Language</u> which plays on the emotions. Often used to persuade or influence the reader.

EMPHASIS (em-fa-sis) is used in <u>poems</u> to give more meaning to the reader. Emphasis stresses the sound of the <u>words</u> to build up a picture in the following ways:

- ◆ by <u>alliteration</u>
- ◆ by <u>assonance</u>
- ◆ by repeating the same words, e.g. *far and few, far and few*
- ◆ by repeating the meaning using different words, e.g. *fast and furious, rant and rave*
- ◆ by using opposites together, e.g. *come and go, here and there, first and last*

ENCYCLOPAEDIA (en-ci-clo-pee-dee-a) A <u>book</u> full of facts, pictures and information about all kinds of subjects and listed in <u>alphabetical order</u>.

ENJAMBMENT When a <u>poem</u> flows from one line to the next without punctuation.

> *"And start and snap at blackbirds bouncing by*
> *To fight and catch the great white butterfly."*
>
> 'The Vixen' by John Clare

EPIC POEM An extended <u>narrative poem</u> recounting actions, travels, adventures and heroic episodes.

> Examples of epic poems include:
>
> '*Iliad*' by Homer
> '*Odyssey*' by Homer
> '*Paradise Lost*' by Milton

EPIGRAM (ep-i-gram) There are two types, poetic and non-poetic.

- *Poetic* A short <u>poem</u> (Poetic Epigram) that ends with a <u>wit</u>ty expression.

> *"Little strokes*
> *Fell great oaks"* - Benjamin Franklin
>
> *"What is an epigram? A dwarfish whole*
> *Its body brevity and wit its soul"* - Samuel Taylor
> Coleridge

- *Non-Poetic* A short witty saying that makes a point.

> *"With friends like you who needs enemies?"*
>
> *"I can resist anything except temptation."* - Oscar Wilde

EPILOGUE (ep-i-log) Appears at the end of a piece of <u>writing</u> to make the ending more definite. Epilogues are often found in <u>plays</u> by William Shakespeare in the form of a short speech used to finish the <u>story</u>.

EPISODE (ep-i-soh-d) An instalment, programme or part of a longer running <u>story</u> usually produced for television or radio.

EPITAPH (ep-i-tarf) A brief <u>poem</u> or other <u>writing</u> in praise, memory or commemorating the life of a person now deceased.

Usually an epitaph appears as an inscription on a tombstone or monument about the person who is buried there.

Whilst sometimes solemn, epitaphs can also express <u>witty</u> sentiments about the deceased.

> In memory of a young man:
>
> *"It was so soon that I was done for*
> *I wonder what I was begun for"*
>
> From a church in Yorkshire:
>
> *"Here Isabel my wife doth lie*
> *She's at peace and so am I"*
>
> In memory of John Snell:
>
> *"Here lie I and no wonder I'm dead*
> *For a wagon wheel ran over my head"*

EPITHET (ep-i-thet) Any <u>word</u> or <u>phrase</u> applied to a person or thing to characterise them or to act as a descriptive substitute for their name or <u>title</u>.

Name/Title	Epithet
King Richard I	*Richard the Lion-Heart*
Abraham Lincoln	*The Great Emancipator*
Florence Nightingale	*The Lady with the Lamp*
A dog	*Man's best friend*

EPONYM (epp-o-nim) A term for a <u>word</u> that is derived from the proper name of a person or place.

"Sandwich" from the Earl of Sandwich
"Pasteurization" from the Louis Pasteur
"Guillotine" from Dr. J.I. Guillotin

ESSAY (es-say) A <u>literary</u> <u>composition</u> set out in an ordinary style. An essay is usually relatively short and can be on any subject.

ETC. is the <u>abbreviation</u> for et cetera which is used to avoid naming lots of examples. It means "and other things", "and the rest", "and so on".

ETYMOLOGY (et-im-ol-oh-jee) The study of how <u>word</u>s are formed and where they came from.

EULOGY (yooh-luh-jee) A formal speech or written tribute expressing high praise or commendation for a character and/or services of someone who has died.

A eulogy can sometimes be used as an address for introducing speakers or nominating candidates.

EUPHEMISM (you-fem-is-um) The use of a mild, vague expression instead of one which might be considered embarrassing, distasteful or unpleasant.

> instead of *died* use:
>
> *passed on, passed away, departed this life*
>
> instead of *toilet* use:
>
> *facilities, bathroom, powder room, little boy's room, loo*

EVALUATE A command word sometimes used in an examination or literacy question. It requires you to consider the information, extract or evidence and to distinguish between relevant facts and opinions. You should then make a judgement of the relative value of what you have considered and write a concluding statement that reflects your assessment and opinion.

EXAGGERATION (ex-adg-er-ray-shun) A technique used in persuasive writing to make points sound better than they really are. A useful technique which makes a point and can also be amusing. (Also see Rhetorical Device.)

> *I've told you a thousand times, don't exaggerate!*
>
> *I've been there hundreds of times, so I should know.*

EXAMINE (ex-am-in) A command word sometimes used in an examination or literacy question. It means you have to consider in detail and analyse a topic to discover particular features or meanings. A concluding evaluative statement may be presented giving an opinion or judgement based upon what has been identified.

EXCLAMATION MARK (ex-clam-a-shun mark) A <u>punctuation mark</u> (!) that acts as a <u>full stop</u> in a <u>sentence</u> or <u>phrase</u> which shows strong feelings such as surprise, pleasure, shock or fear, e.g. *Be quiet!, Oh no!, Come here!*

♦ Exclamation marks can also be used after an <u>interjection</u>, e.g. *Ouch!, Oh!, Ah!*

♦ Exclamation marks should be used appropriately in <u>writing</u> to create impact for the reader.

♦ It is unnecessary to write more than one exclamation mark at a time, tempting though it may be!

EXCLAMATION (ex-clam-a-shun) (See also Exclamation Mark.) <u>Sentence</u>s or <u>phrase</u>s which state a command or express strong feelings or emotions, e.g. *Go now!, Stop that!, Well done!*

Exclamations are followed by an <u>exclamation mark</u>.

EXEUNT (ex-you-ant) A <u>word</u> used in <u>stage directions</u> to show that more than one person has left the stage.

EXPLAIN A <u>command word</u> sometimes used in an examination or <u>literacy</u> <u>question</u>. It means you have to make clear and understandable something that may be unclear or not well understood. You may need to set out reasons for a cause or event or to justify actions, beliefs or remarks to make clear what, how or why something has occurred.

EXPLORE A <u>command word</u> sometimes used in an examination or <u>literacy</u> <u>question</u>. It means you have to look into something closely. You may have to search out, <u>investigate</u> and inquire into something with the aim of discovering some important points or features about the subject. A concluding written statement will <u>highlight</u> the main things identified.

EXPOSITION (ex-spuh-zish-uhn) The part of a <u>story structure</u> that provides the reader with the <u>setting</u> of the <u>story</u>, situation (time and place) and introduces the <u>characters</u>.

EXTRACT A short piece of <u>text</u> taken from a longer piece of <u>writing</u>. Extracts of stories are often used as the basis for <u>comprehension</u> exercises.

FABLE (fay-bul) A <u>short story</u> written and told to make a point and with a moral behind it, e.g. *The Tortoise and the Hare*.

FAIRY TALE A traditional <u>story</u> told and written to entertain children. These are well known and often include:

- a simple beginning, e.g. *"Once upon a time"* or *"In a land far away"*

- a mix of characters, e.g. *animals, children, royalty, stepmothers, elves, dwarves, fairies, pixies, witches, etc.*

- a <u>theme</u> of good against evil

- a happy ending, e.g. *"and they all lived happily ever after"*

FALLING ACTION The part of the <u>story structure</u> following the <u>crisis</u> where the results and outcomes of the <u>conflict</u> are revealed.

FANTASY STORY (fan-tas-see stor-ee) An imaginary adventure <u>story</u> which has a magical <u>theme</u>. The <u>setting</u> can be either:

- an imaginary world where fantastic things happen

- the real world where strange and amazing things happen

FARCE (far-se) <u>Literature</u> or <u>drama</u> that combines ludicrous incidents, an improbable <u>plot</u> and stereotyped <u>characters</u> to achieve <u>humour</u>.

> Examples of farce includes:
>
> '*The Importance of Being Earnest*' by Oscar Wilde
>
> '*Private Lives*' by Noel Coward

Farce sometimes has an underlying satirical message that aims to make a point.

FEMININE NOUN (fem-in-in nown) (See Gender.)

FICTION (fick-shun) A <u>story</u>, <u>novel</u>, <u>play</u> or <u>poem</u> that is not real. The people and things that happen are imaginary and are made up by the writer. Fiction contrasts with <u>non-fiction</u> <u>writing</u>.

FIGURATIVE LANGUAGE (fig-uh-ra-tiv lang-gwi-j) <u>Language</u> where the intended meaning differs from the actual literal meaning of the <u>words</u> themselves. Figurative language uses imaginative, non-literal words and <u>phrases</u> that make <u>writing</u> stronger and more effective. Figurative writing is the opposite of <u>literal writing</u> and is used to give the reader a mind picture of what the writer is trying to say.

> Doug is a real *live wire.*
> (meaning Doug is active and always on the move. It
>   has nothing to do with electricity!)
>
> "All the world's *a stage*" from the play 'As You Like It'
>   by William Shakespeare.
>
> The road was a *silver river*, the moon a *golden pool.*
>
> Don drove *like a maniac.*

Figurative language is often associated with literature and poetry in particular. Poets often use figurative language and when you read poetry you should be aware of the difference from literal writing or the poem will not make sense.

A comparison or exaggeration used to create figurative language is known as a figure of speech.

FIGURE OF SPEECH (fig-uh ov sp-ee-ch)   A literary device that achieves a special effect by arranging words and sounds in distinctive ways. Using figures of speech can make writing more interesting, lively and powerful by creating word associations that enhance, emphasise, beautify and embellish writing. There are many figures of speech but the most commonly used are allegory, alliteration, allusion, analogy, antithesis, cliché, colloquialism, ellipsis, epigram, euphemism, hyperbole, irony, litotes, metaphor, metonym, onomatopoeia, oxymoron, paradox, personification, proverb, pun, rhetorical question, sarcasm, satire, simile, slang, symbol, zeugma.

FIRST PERSON (Also see Conjugation.) The grammatical form adopted by a speaker or writer referring to herself or himself. Examples of forms in the first person include English pronouns such as *I, me* and *we.*

It is also the writing style used if you are the character or narrator in the story recounting her or his own experiences or impressions.

> A character in a novel written in the first person might say:
>
> *I walked down the street.*
>
> *I typed on my computer.*

FLASHBACK A <u>writing</u> technique in which the <u>author</u> interrupts the <u>plot</u> of the <u>story</u> to recreate an incident that occurred at an earlier time. This can be done by taking <u>characters</u> back to the beginning of the <u>tale</u>. This technique is used to provide additional information for the reader.

FOIL (foy-al) A <u>character</u> in a work of <u>literature</u> who serves as a contrast to another character (usually the <u>protagonist</u>). The foil's character portrays characteristics, values and ideas that are different from or opposed to the other character. This enables the reader to make judgements and comparisons between them.

> In 'Macbeth' by William Shakespeare, the character MacDuff is portrayed as a noble and virtuous father and provides an ideal foil for the dishonourable, murderous, childless Macbeth.

FONT A term now often used as a <u>metonym</u> for typeface, typically the size and shape of <u>letters</u>, <u>characters</u> and <u>symbols</u>.

FOOTNOTE A short explanation, usually at the foot of a page and accompanied by an <u>asterisk</u>, which refers to a <u>word</u> or point made in a piece of <u>text</u>.

FOREIGN WORDS & PHRASES (fawr-in words and fray-zes) Words and phrases in another language used in the English <u>language</u>. Often <u>author</u>s use these expressions for effect.

carpe diem (Latin)	⇒	seize the day
terra firma (Latin)	⇒	solid ground
dolce vita (Italian)	⇒	good life
vox pop (Latin)	⇒	voice of the people
schadenfreude (German)	⇒	laughter at another's expense
joie de vivre (French)	⇒	a feeling of healthy enjoyment of life

FORESHADOWING   A <u>writing</u> technique where future events in a <u>story</u> or even the outcome are suggested by the <u>author</u> before they happen. The author provides clues or hints as to what is going to happen later in the story.

FORMAL LETTER   A <u>letter</u> with often serious <u>content</u> (rather than an affectionate communication) which is written to someone in their professional capacity and who may not be well known to the writer. A formal letter might request information, accompany something that is sent as a general mailshot, or be a letter of complaint.

Some conventions that apply to formal letters written in English are:

- your address should be written in the top right hand corner of the letter

- the address of the person you are writing to (the addressee) should be written on the left, set below your address

- the date can be written either on the right hand side under your address or on the left hand side under the address you are writing to with the month written as a <u>word</u>

- the salutation or greeting should begin with "Dear" followed by the addressee's name. Use the title Mr, Mrs, Miss or Ms, Dr, <u>etc</u>. and the surname only. For women, where marital status is unknown use Ms. which is for both married and single woman.

- if the addresses's name is not known, begin with "Dear Sir/Madam". It is advisable to try to give a name and title if you can.

- between the salutation and the body of the letter it is customary to give a heading, being a reference or short indication of the purpose of the letter, and this should be <u>highlight</u>ed in bold and/or underlined

- the first <u>paragraph</u> should be short and state the purpose of the letter, e.g. to complain, request something or make an enquiry

- the following paragraph(s) should contain the relevant information behind the writing of the letter. This information should be concise, clear, logical and well organised.

- the final paragraph should state what action you expect the recipient of the letter to take, e.g. to send information, to investigate a complaint, to refund money, etc.

- use "Yours faithfully" to end a letter where the addressee's name is not known

- use "Yours sincerely" to end a letter where the addressee's name is known

- sign your name and then print it below your signature

- put your title in brackets after your name

Formal letters contrast with Informal Letters.

FORMAL WRITING Writing that is usually impersonal and addresses a general audience about a range of things and often uses the present tense. Formal writing is used for essays, assignments or other academic works. It follows certain conventions. It is advisable **not** to use:

- abbreviations

- cliches

- contractions

- extra words, e.g. *well, you know*

- first person, e.g. *I, we, my, us*

- second person, e.g. *you, your, yours*

- unnecessary words, e.g. *very, really* as in "it was *really, very* important"

- etc. – in formal writing you need to state all there is to say and not allude to it by using "etc."

It is advisable **to** use:

- titles – make a title look interesting by putting it in bold or in italics or underlining it

- the third person grammatical form, e.g. *he, she, it, they*

- a clear opening statement of the main idea or thesis

- quotations – ensure you credit the source

- numbers written out, e.g. *"ten"* not *"10"*, although longer numbers and dates may be written numerically, e.g. *2008, £1760.50*

- word choices that are specific, precise and convey the sense of meaning that you intend

- paragraphing to identify, separate and emphasise each significant point you make

- drafting to ensure that your work is coherent

- proofreading to check your work for accuracy

- pagination for orderly progression of your work

- Standard English to ensure that your writing is grammatically correct

FORUM THEATRE (for-um thee-a-ter)   A piece of improvised drama enacted within a group setting where there is the opportunity for interaction between those acting and those observing.

The action may be interrupted, discussed and reworked following what has been discussed. It is a useful technique for considering the different options available to develop the drama.

FREE VERSE is the style used by many modern poets which doesn't use regular rhyme or metre. Although rhyme may be used it is just without a pattern. Free verse poetry is characterised by words and images rather than by regular metrical schemes.

FREEZE FRAME (See Tableaux.)

FULL STOP (also called a period) is the strongest <u>punctuation</u> <u>mark</u> and is written as a dot (.) at the end of all <u>sentences</u> that are not <u>questions</u> or <u>exclamations</u>.

♦ <u>Question marks</u> (?) and <u>exclamation marks</u> (!) carry their own full stops so you do not need to put an extra one after using these punctuation marks.

♦ Full stops are used in a row of three (<u>ellipsis</u>) to show that a part of a <u>quotation</u> or <u>text</u> has been left out.

♦ Full stops can also be used after <u>abbreviations</u> where words have been shortened or where <u>letters</u> have been left out.

Feb. 19th	(February 19th)
Capt.	(Captain)
Prof.	(Professor)

FUNCTIONAL LITERACY (funk-shun-al lit-er-a-see) (Also see Literacy.) A term used in modern contexts to refer to reading and <u>writing</u> levels adequate to enable communication and understanding to take place in a society that is literate.

FUTURE PERFECT TENSE (Also see Conjugation.) A verb tense used to describe action that will be completed in the future, e.g. *I will have walked.*

FUTURE TENSE (Also see Conjugation.) A verb tense that expresses actions in the future, e.g. *I will/shall walk.*

GENDER (jen-der) The form that a <u>noun</u> takes, whether masculine (male), feminine (female), common or neuter (without a sex). Words which are common <u>gender</u> can be either masculine or feminine.

Masculine	Feminine	Neuter	Common
father	mother	table	teacher
uncle	aunt	chair	player
nephew	niece	weather	runner

GENRE (jon-ra) The different kinds or types of stories. In <u>literature</u>, this could include mystery, detective, <u>science fiction</u>, historical, thriller, romance, fantasy, horror or humorous.

GERUND (jer-uhnd) is when the <u>present participle</u> is used as a <u>noun</u>.

> The *chattering* of the class annoyed the teacher.

A gerund acts like any other noun and so can be described by an <u>adjective</u>.

> The *awful chattering* of the class annoyed the teacher.

(Like any other noun, you can put 'the' in front of it.)

GLOSSARY (gloss-a-ree) An explanation of new or difficult <u>word</u>s in a piece of <u>writing</u>.

GOBBLEDYGOOK (gob-al-dee-gook) A term used to describe nonsensical <u>language</u> which conveys no intelligible meaning. It is often used to describe incomprehensible or pompous <u>jargon</u> used by specialists.

GRAFFITI (gruh-fee-tee) A drawing, marking, initials, slogan or inscription that is made by spray painting or <u>writing</u> on a wall or other surface where it can be viewed by the public.

GRAMMAR Rules and guidelines that we use in <u>language</u> (both spoken and written) so that we can clearly express what we mean and so that what we say and write can be properly understood.

GROUP TERM (Also known as Collective Noun.)

HACKNEYED (hack-need) A name given to an expression that has been repeated too often and has therefore become over familiar through overuse, e.g. *frail grannies, disgraced politician, innocent victims, police crackdown, lifestyle choice, legendary actor, mammoth income.*

HAIKU (hi-koo) (Also see Japanese Poetry.) A form of short, simple <u>poetry</u> that originated in Japan. It does not need to <u>rhyme</u> but it must have 17 <u>syllables</u> in a fixed pattern: line 1 has 5 syllables, line 2 has 7 syllables and line 3 has 5 syllables. Often the subject of haiku is nature. Haiku <u>poem</u>s can be used to create beautiful word pictures.

	<u>syllables</u>
Leaves now flutter down	5
Falling from the bare branches	7
Autumn has arrived	5

HALF-RHYME (harf-rime) Words that have almost the same pattern of <u>vowels</u> and <u>consonant</u>s at the end and may nearly <u>rhyme</u>, e.g. *sun – tan, kilt – felt.*

HEADLINE (hed-line) The <u>text</u> at the top of a <u>newspaper article</u> that indicates what the <u>article</u> below is about. Headlines are usually written in bold and in a much larger <u>font</u> size than the <u>article</u> <u>text</u>. Front page headlines are often in <u>upper case</u> so that they can be read easily by potential customers.

HIGHLIGHT (hi-lite) To pick out or identify <u>key words</u>, terms or <u>phrases</u> from a piece of <u>text</u> in order to emphasise, illustrate or support a point being made. Highlighting may involve using quotation marks, underlining or colouring with a highlighter pen to draw attention to the key words.

HISTORIES (hist-or-ees) <u>Plays</u> based on real history, e.g. *'Henry V'* and *'Julius Caesar'* by William Shakespeare.

HOMOGRAPH (hom-oh-graf) Words which are identical in <u>spelling</u> but different in meaning and usually <u>pronunciation</u>.

Word	Meaning	Pronunciation
sow	female pig	sou
sow	scatter seed	soh
bow	front of a ship	bou
bow	weapon fires an arrow	boh
sewer	pipe for waste disposal	soo-er
sewer	person who sews cloth	soh-er

HOMONYM (hom-oh-nim) Words which are spelt the same and sound the same as another word but have different meanings.

> The noun *bear* (animal).
> The verb *bear* (to carry).
>
> The noun *bank* (embankment).
> The noun *bank* (depository for money).
>
> The noun *fan* (as in football fan).
> The verb *fan* (to waft air).

> The footballer was sent off for a *foul*.
> The water tasted *foul*.
>
> The boy complained that it wasn't *fair*.
> We all won prizes when we went to the *fair*.

HOMOPHONES (hom-oh-fones) Words that have the same sound but different meanings and <u>spelling</u>s.

> *pear*   (fruit)
> *pare*   (to cut off)
> *pair*   (two of a kind)
>
> *rain*   (water droplets)
> *rein*   (to guide a horse)
> *reign*   (duration of a monarch's rule)

> The girl used her *right* hand to *write* the letter.
> We stood on the beach so we could *see* the *sea*.

HOT SEATING A <u>drama</u> convention where a person assumes the <u>role</u> of one of the <u>characters</u> in the drama and is then questioned by other members of the group. The aim is to probe the character's motives, attitudes and behaviour.

HUMOUR (hume-er) A technique used in speaking and <u>writing</u> to emphasise a point or to grab the <u>audience</u>'s attention and keep them listening by amusing them. Humour can involve using a joke or <u>anecdote</u> to make or illustrate a point.

HYPERBOLE (hi-per-boh-lee) Overstatement or <u>exaggeration</u> for effect. It is often used humorously to make a point.

> "I've told you a thousand times, don't exaggerate!"
>
> "She will kill me if I'm late again"

HYPHEN (hi-fen) A shorter line than a <u>dash</u>. It is a <u>punctuation mark</u> used to link two words together to make one word or expression, e.g. *hitch-hike, self-service, dry-clean*.

HYPOTHESIS (hi-poth-ess-iss) A theory (an idea) that has not been proven. A hypothesis usually takes the form of a <u>statement</u> or <u>question</u> that can be the subject of investigation.

IAMBIC PENTAMETER (i-am-bick pent-am-ee-ter) The <u>metre</u> found in <u>blank verse</u> where each line has ten <u>syllables</u>, five of them stressed and five unstressed. Many of Shakespeare's <u>plays</u> contain this metre.

IDIOM (id-ee-um) A <u>phrase</u> that is not meant literally. It suggests an idea or message which is disguised within words that, taken literally, mean something else. To understand an idiom you need to know the message behind it.

"to take take the wind out of your sails"
– to say something that effectively undermines someone's argument

"to pour cold water over something"
– to say that something won't work or to say that an idea is no good

"back to square one"
– to start again

"new kid on the block"
– a newcomer to the neighbourhood

IMAGERY (im-er-jree) A <u>word</u> or words which create a mental picture.

Three ways of creating an image or a mind picture for the reader when <u>writing</u> <u>poetry</u> or <u>prose</u> are:

◆ <u>similies</u>

◆ <u>metaphors</u>

◆ <u>personification</u>

IMPERATIVE (im-pair-a-tiv) (See Command Sentence.)

IMPERSONAL WRITING A <u>style of writing</u> in the <u>present tense</u> that uses <u>passive verbs</u> to talk about people in general rather than as individuals.

IMPROVISATION (im-pro-vi-za-shun) A technique used in <u>drama</u> which involves the planned or spontaneous development of a <u>script</u> or <u>structure</u>. Improvisation can provide opportunities for the drama to develop in different directions as agreed by those involved.

INDEFINITE ARTICLE (in-def-in-ate ar-tick-al) The words 'a' or 'an' used in a <u>sentence</u> to give a different meaning to the <u>nouns</u> that follow them. They are used when no particular thing or <u>object</u> is required and one out of any number will do.

Use *an* in front of a word that begins with a <u>vowel</u>. Use *a* in front of a word that begins with a <u>consonant</u>.

Some exceptions are where the first <u>letter</u> in a word is a <u>silent letter</u> but is followed by a <u>vowel</u> so the word sounds as if it begins with a vowel, e.g. *an hour, an honour.*

INDEFINITE PRONOUN (in-def-in-ate pro-nown) (See Pronoun.)

INDENT The process of moving <u>text</u> horizontally away from the <u>margin</u> to set it apart from the surrounding text, as in the first line of a <u>paragraph</u>.

INDEPENDENT CLAUSE (Also known as a Main Clause.)

INDEX The last pages in a <u>book</u> containing lists of important words set out in <u>alphabetical order</u> and page numbers where they can be found.

INDEX WORDS The two <u>word</u>s in bold <u>letters</u> found at the top of each page in a <u>dictionary</u>. They indicate the first and last words on the page and help you find where the word you are looking for is.

INDIRECT QUESTION A <u>sentence</u> which does not ask a <u>question</u> but tells you what question was asked. It does not need an answer and does not have a <u>question mark</u>.

> *He asked how many goals were scored.*
>
> *She asked how you were.*
>
> *He asked what the date was.*

Indirect questions can also be a subtle way of eliciting information without being too specific.

> The bank clerk asked, *"How do you like your money?"*
>
> Irene replied, *"Very much, thank you."*
>
> - the expected response to this question would be, *"In 10s and 20 pound notes, please"*.

INDIRECT SPEECH (See Reported Speech.)

INFINITIVE The simple, basic form of a <u>verb</u>, e.g. *go, walk, sleep, think, fly*.

Often the word "to" marks a verb as an infinitive, e.g. *to go, to walk, to sleep, to think, to fly.*

INFLECTION (in-fleck-shun) A change in the form of a word (usually by adding a <u>prefix</u> or <u>suffix</u>) to indicate a change in its grammatical function.

Singular noun	Plural noun	
dog	dogs	suffix 's' added
Present tense	**Past tense**	
walk	walked	suffix 'ed' added
Noun	**Verb**	
slave	enslave	prefix 'en' added

INFORMAL LETTER A <u>letter</u> that is written to people known well to the writer. The <u>style of writing</u> is often chatty, informal, sometimes amusing, and may be written as you might speak to a friend.

Informal letters may be written to thank or compliment someone, to share news or just to say hello and keep in touch. Informal letters, written by hand, are considered to be the most personal.

Some conventions that apply to informal letters written in English are:

- it is usual to write only your address at the top right hand side of the letter

- write the date underneath the address

- begin the letter in a friendly, personal way using the greeting "Dear" followed by the person's first name, e.g. *Dear Louise...*

- the first/introductory paragraph should explain the purpose for your writing and need only be brief, personal and honest

- the main body of the letter can be written in a conversational tone. It could be setting out information in order or if you have a number of things to say use first, secondly, etc. so that the reader can share and follow your thought processes easily.

- the closing paragraph can invite the reader to write back, stay in touch, pass on good wishes or similar sentiments

Informal letters sign off with a personal touch using, e.g. *Kind regards, Write soon, Miss you, All the best, Best wishes* or *Love from*. The writer may just use their first name to sign off at the end.

Informal letters contrast with Formal Letters.

INFORMAL WRITING is used for the many forms of writing not considered to be formal writing and where quality of writing and creative writing skills need to be particularly demonstrated. Informal writing should/can:

- represent a sense of the author's personality in order to make the writing unique and special

- display evidence of original thoughts and ideas

- reveal a personal perspective to what is written and convey this to the reader

- set out to entertain, captivate and persuade the reader with the vision enshrined in the writing

- be free from the conventions required by Standard English

- employ First, Second or Third Person grammatical forms

INITIALISM (i-nish-el-izam) An abbreviation consisting of initial letters of words. The convention is usually not to separate the individual letters with full stops.

BBC	*– British Broadcasting Corporation*
ITN	*– Independent Television News*
FA	*– Football Association*
YHA	*– Youth Hostel Association*

INTERJECTION (in-ter-jeck-shun) One of the nine Parts of Speech. A word used to express exclamation, e.g. *Oh!, Hello!, Hooray!, Hey!*

INTERNAL RHYME is where words in the middle of a line rhyme with those at the beginning and end of a line too.

> She tried so hard to *block* the *knock,*
>
> That woke her from a *sleep* so *deep.*
>
> More *furious* than *curious,*
>
> Feet smote the *floor* to reach the *door*

INTERROGATIVE PRONOUN (in-tare-ro-gay-tiv pro-nown) (See Pronoun.)

INTONATION (in-toh-nay-shun) A variation of pitch in the voice when speaking. The way the sound of a voice changes especially in relation to what is being spoken. Intonation may vary between questions, statements or to convey irony or surprise.

A conversation can illustrate this:

Louise fell out of the tree.	(statement)
She did what?	(question expressing surprise)
She fell out of the tree.	(statement)
What was she doing up a tree?	(question expressing indignation)
She was trying to pick apples.	(statement)
Not the cleverest thing to do.	(statement expressed ironically)

INVECTIVE (in-veck-tiv) Speech or writing that is severely reproachful and abuses, denounces or attacks. It can be directed against a person, cause, idea or system. It employs a heavy use of negative, emotive language.

INVERTED COMMAS (See Speech Marks.)

INVESTIGATE A command word sometimes used in an examination or literacy question. It means you have to observe, examine or make a detailed inquiry into something with care and accuracy. A concluding written statement will set out the results and findings of your investigation.

IRONY (i-ron-ee) An ironic tone is used in poetry and prose when a writer says one thing but it is clear that they mean something very different, perhaps the exact opposite.

The famous opening of Jane Austen's *'Pride and Prejudice'* is ironic. It states:

"It is a truth universally acknowledged, that a single man in possession of a good fortune must be in want of a wife."

It actually means that although society believed this to be true, many single men would disagree.

(Also see Dramatic Irony, Situational Irony and Verbal Irony.)

ITALICS (it-al-icks) A style of <u>font</u> using sloping <u>letters</u> developed in Italy in the 16th century and now used to give emphasis or distinction to words.

JAPANESE POETRY Short and simple <u>poems</u> that do not have to <u>rhyme</u> and which follow a regular pattern of <u>syllables</u> and lines. <u>Haiku</u>, <u>tanka</u> and <u>renga</u> are all examples of Japanese <u>poetry</u>.

JARGON Technical words and terms that are specifically related to a particular topic. Jargon words and terms may only be understood by people familiar with the topic and a reader unfamiliar with the topic may have difficulty making sense of them, e.g. in tennis, *'a let'*, *'love fifteen'* and *'deuce'* are all jargon.

JINGLE (jing-gel) A short catchy <u>poem</u> or <u>song</u> which is used in advertising. Jingles are designed to make you associate a particular product with the <u>rhyme</u> or <u>song</u>. To work well, jingles either use rhyming words or <u>alliteration</u>.

JOURNALIST (jurn-al-ist) A writer or reporter who uses <u>journalistic writing</u> and who writes <u>article</u>s for newspapers and magazines.

JOURNALISTIC WRITING (jurn-al-is-tick ri-ting) A <u>style of writing</u> used in <u>newspapers</u> and <u>magazines</u> with the aim of entertaining and informing readers and which <u>comment</u>s on, and includes, facts and news.

The style often uses <u>passive verbs</u>, an impersonal <u>tone</u>, persuasive and <u>emotive language</u> and <u>phrase</u>s and <u>clause</u>s inserted between two <u>comma</u>s to provide extra information.

JUXTAPOSITION (juhk-stuh-puh-zi-shun) When the <u>author</u> places two items, <u>themes</u>, <u>phrases</u>, <u>words</u>, <u>characters</u> or situations together side by side to create a certain effect for comparison or contrast.

> wealth and poverty
>
> rich and poor
>
> guilt and innocence
>
> generosity and greed
>
> heaven and hell

KENNING A description often used in <u>poetry</u> to describe someone or something without actually naming them.

heart-breaker	an attractive person
dream-chaser	an idealist
fly-catcher	spider
tree-climber, bin-raider ⎤ *food-hider, nut-cracker* ⎦	squirrel

KEYWORD (kee-wurd) A <u>word</u> used as a reference point for finding other words or information. It is a feature which is used to search for linked information on databases, in <u>documents</u> and through internet search engines.

> You could search the database for the keyword
>
> "Tutor Master"

KEY WORDS (kee wurds) appear in a <u>question</u> that needs a written answer. When answering a question it is important to address the key words in particular and to make sure that it is clear to the examiner that this has been done. (Also see Command Words.)

> *How* does the *writer* try to *build up excitement* and *suspense throughout* this passage?

LAMENT A <u>poem</u> expressing sorrow, grief, regret or mourning, usually over a death of a loved one.

LAMPOON A crude, coarse, often bitter <u>satire</u>, ridiculing the personal appearance or character of a person. Lampoon is both a <u>noun</u> and a <u>verb</u>.

LANDSCAPE Used in the <u>layout</u> or framing of <u>text</u> or pictures where the horizontal width of the frame is longer than the vertical height of the frame. It is derived from the horizontal rectangular layout of a traditional classical landscape painting. The opposite layout is known as <u>portrait</u>.

LANGUAGE (lang-gwi-dge) The communication system used by humans consisting of written or spoken words.

The speech of a country, region or group of people including its <u>vocabulary</u>, <u>syntax</u> and <u>grammar</u>.

LANGUAGE IN TEXTS (lang-gwi-dge in texts) A broad area of <u>literary</u> study which covers topics such as:

- how the <u>vocabulary</u> is used and whether it is simple or complicated, detailed or factual.

- whether changes occur in the <u>language</u> between different parts of the <u>text</u> and any reasons for this.

- how <u>characters</u> speak in a text and what this tells about them, i.e. rich, poor, foreign. Is <u>dialect</u> a feature of their language?

LAYOUT The way that a text is presented, e.g. dictionaries use <u>alphabetical order</u>, formal <u>letters</u> are set out with dates, addresses and endings presented in a particular way.

Layout is the way that the individual parts of a <u>document</u> are set out to create the best visual impact and to communicate information effectively to the reader. (See Landscape and Portrait.)

LEAFLET A single sheet of paper or card that is used to communicate information about a topic or event in a direct and straightforward way. The production of a leaflet should consider:

- design
- layout
- easy readability
- use of pictures
- catchy slogans

- diagrams
- imaginative use of font size and style
- bullet points
- use of colour

LEGEND (ledge-end) A traditional story based on the lives of real people which began as true stories but have been added to, exaggerated, embellished or romanticised since.

> *The Legend of Robin Hood and his Merry Men.*
>
> *The Legend of Dick Whittington and his cat.*

LETTER A written or printed communication addressed to a person or an organisation and usually posted and delivered by mail. (Also see Formal and Informal Letter.)

LETTERS The symbols used in writing to create words. Together they comprise the alphabet. The English alphabet is made up of twenty-six letters. Five of these letters are called vowels. Twenty-one of these letters are called consonants.

LEXICON (lecks-ee-con) A reference book containing an alphabetical list of words with information, e.g. *a dictionary* or *thesaurus.* Also the vocabulary that is used by a person, profession, social group, subject or language.

LIMERICK (lim-er-ick) A funny <u>poem</u> that usually begins with "There was an old man from..." or something similar. There is always a place name in the first line. The <u>rhyme scheme</u> is A-A-B-B-A with three stressed beats in the A lines and two stressed beats in the B lines.

	<u>Rhyme scheme</u>
There was an old man from Cosham	A
Who took out his false teeth to wash 'em	A
His wife said, "Now Jack,	B
If you don't put 'em back	B
I'll tread on your gnashers and squash 'em	A
Anon.	

LINK WORD A word, such as *who*, *which*, *that* and *whom*, used to link two <u>sentences</u>.

♦ Use *who* and *whom* for people

There is the boy *who* scored the goal.

I met a lady *whom* I knew.

♦ Use *which* for things

There is a door *which* never closes.

♦ Use *that* for people or things

Here are the people and bags *that* arrived late.

LINKING PHRASE (link-ing fray-ze) is used when answering a <u>question</u> to help join all the points being made.

> *On the other hand, ...*
>
> *In conclusion, ...*
>
> *It has also been suggested that, ...*

LINKING WORD (See Conjunction.)

LITOTES (lie-tote-ease) An <u>understatement</u> usually achieved by using a <u>double negative</u> to convey the opposite meaning.

> *They are not a bad team.*
>
> [meaning : They are a good team.]
>
> *Snakes are not the safest creatures to keep as pets.*
>
> [meaning : Snakes are quite dangerous to
>
> keep as pets.]
>
> *It's not uncomplicated.*
>
> [meaning : It is complicated.]

LITERACY (lit-er-a-see) (Also see Functional Literacy.) The traditional <u>definition</u> of literacy is considered to be the ability to read and write. An extended definition includes the ability to use <u>language</u> to read, write, listen and speak.

LITERAL WRITING <u>Writing</u> that expresses exactly what the writer means and is factually correct in every detail.

LITERARY (lit-uh-rer-ee) Relating to all aspects of <u>literature</u>, e.g. *books, poems, writing, letters, etc.*

LITERARY CRITICISM (lit-uh-rer-ee crit-ih-sis-um) is the study, discussion, evaluation and interpretation of <u>literature</u>.

LITERATURE (lit-rich-er) Creative <u>writing</u> that is generally considered to have artistic value and is distinguished for beauty of style or expression as in <u>poetry</u>, <u>essays</u>, <u>novellas</u> and <u>novels</u>.

LONG STOP (See Punctuation Mark.)

LOWER CASE LETTERS (See Alphabet.)

LYRIC POEM (lih-rick po-em) A short <u>poem</u> with <u>song</u>-like qualities and intensity of expression. Lyric poems often tell of the <u>poet</u>'s innermost thoughts and state of mind. Originally they were sung to the music of a lyre.

Sonnets, <u>odes</u> and <u>elegies</u> are all lyric poems.

LYRICS (lih-ricks) The written <u>text</u> (i.e. the words) of a <u>song</u>.

MAGAZINE (mag-a-zeen) tends to be produced either monthly or weekly and it focuses on providing <u>articles</u>, news and features on a particular subject or <u>theme</u>. Magazines are written for a particular <u>audience</u>, e.g. *Motor sports, Football, Healthy Living, House Interiors* or *Gardening*.

MAIN CLAUSE (See Clause.)

MALAPROPISM (mal-a-prop-is-em) The use of an incorrect <u>word</u> which may have a similar sound or <u>spelling</u> to the correct word that was intended.

eliminate and *illuminate*

The soldiers were ordered to *illuminate* the enemy.

monogamy and *monotony*

Having only one husband or wife is known as *monotony*.

MANUSCRIPT The original <u>text</u> of an <u>author</u>'s work, handwritten or now usually typed, that is submitted to a publisher for publication.

MARGIN The space around the edge or border of a piece of <u>text</u> usually marked by a line. The margin can be used to write brief <u>notes</u> or to identify and separate points with <u>letters</u> or numbers. <u>Paragraphs</u> can be identified by being <u>indent</u>ed from the margin.

MEDIA (mee-di-a) The different ways that information and news is presented to us, e.g. *television, radio, newspapers, magazines* and *internet*.

MEIOSIS (my-o-sis) (Also known as an Understatement.) A <u>rhetorical device</u> used in <u>writing</u> and language for effect or to imply that something is less in significance or size than it really is.

> *"The Troubles"* to describe the social, political and religious strife in Northern Ireland.
>
> *"Buck House"* for the name of Buckingham Palace.
>
> *"The Pond"* as a name for the Atlantic Ocean.

METAPHOR (metta-for) (Also see Rhetorical Device.) A <u>phrase</u> or <u>sentence</u> which compares two things by saying that something **is** something else.

> The moon *is a big lump of yellow cheese.*
>
> She *is full of beans.*
>
> He *is a real live wire.*

A metaphor is different from a <u>simile</u> because you do not use 'like' or 'as'.

METONYM (metto-nim) A <u>word</u> that denotes one thing but refers to a related thing. A metonym is a <u>figure of speech</u> and is similar to a <u>metaphor</u> in that one word may be used in place of another. The difference is that a metonym works by association between two concepts whereas a metaphor works by the similarity between them.

plastic	⇒	credit card
Downing Street	⇒	British Government
The White House	⇒	American Government
The Press	⇒	reporters
The Crown	⇒	the monarch

METRE (mee-ter) The <u>rhythm</u> of the lines in a <u>poem</u> based on the number and the pattern of stressed and unstressed <u>syllable</u>s.

MIME (myme) A performance acted without <u>word</u>s but with facial expressions, gestures and bodily movements only.

MIND-MAPPING (Also known as Brainstorm or Thought Shower.) A creative process usually involving a group of people in discussion with the aim of giving a wide variety of thoughts and ideas on an issue or <u>question</u>. Mind-mapping is often the first stage in developing an idea.

MIXED METAPHOR (mixed metta-for) A <u>metaphor</u> compares two things by saying that one thing **is** really something else. A mixed metaphor takes the comparison too far so that it becomes confusing.

The following examples illustrate two ways that metaphors can be mixed causing confusion.

He was *a small fish in a big pond.*

He was *a small cog in a big wheel.*

The two above are metaphors and mean that the person was playing a minor role in a bigger situation, but mixing them gives:

He was *a small fish in a big wheel.*

which is confusing.

Sometimes including two metaphors in the same sentence can also confuse the meaning.

After Vicki was saved, Ruth *was over the moon* and came home *walking on air.*

MNEMONIC (nem-on-ic) A <u>sentence</u> that is often amusing and is made up to help you remember something important. It uses the first <u>letter</u> of the <u>word</u>s of the sentence as a cue to recall important words.

North	*Naughty*		*Never*
East	*Elephants*	*or*	*Eat*
South	*Squirt*		*Shredded*
West	*Water*		*Wheat*

MONOLOGUE (mon-oh-log) A <u>play</u> with a cast of one character who tells the whole <u>story</u>.

Also a part of a <u>drama</u> in which a single <u>actor</u> speaks alone usually for a long time and in a dramatic way. (See also Soliloquy.)

MOOD The general sense or feeling which is generated by the <u>text</u>. The reader may have a sense or feeling about the <u>atmosphere</u> or emotional condition created by the writer.

In '*Macbeth*' by William Shakespeare, the mood is dark and mysterious creating a sense of fear and uncertainty.

MORAL LESSON (Also known as a Practical Lesson.) The <u>tale</u> that the <u>author</u> tells behind the <u>story</u> or <u>play</u> and which leaves an impression on the reader. Moral lessons may be conveyed with intent by the author but their assimilation by the reader is based upon a perception and interpretation of the tale which is both subjective and personal.

> '*A Christmas Carol*' by Charles Dickens warns of the dangers of avarice and greed as personified by Scrooge. It shows how a change of heart can lead to a life of generosity, goodwill and joy.
>
> '*To Kill a Mockingbird*' by N. Harper Lee warns of the evil and immoral effects of prejudice in a small community in the Southern USA. The book promotes the ideas of equality and justice for all.
>
> '*Macbeth*' by William Shakespeare warns of the seductive attractions of greed, ambition and power and how succumbing to the desire for these can bring about destruction.

MOTIF In <u>literature</u>, a term that denotes a recurring important idea or image. A motif can be expressed as a single <u>word</u>, <u>phrase</u>, character type or object.

> In '*Macbeth*' by William Shakespeare, the most significant motif is blood, but others include visions and hallucinations.

MYTH (mi-th) A <u>story</u> told since ancient times. Myths are made-up stories about heroes and gods.

NARRATIVE (nar-uh-tiv) Tells the events that happen in a story, <u>poem</u> or by spoken <u>word</u>, in the right order. It can be <u>fiction</u> or something that really happened. It can be spoken or written by the <u>narrator</u>.

NARRATIVE HOOK (nar-uh-tiv hook) The opening part of a <u>story</u> that "hooks" the reader's attention so that they will keep reading.

NARRATIVE POEM (nar-uh-tiv poh-em) A <u>poem</u> that tells a <u>story</u>.

> Some examples of narrative poems are:
>
> *'The Charge of the Light Brigade'* by Alfred Lord Tennyson
>
> *'The Rime of the Ancient Mariner'* by Samuel Taylor Coleridge
>
> *'Venus and Adonis'* by William Shakespeare

NARRATIVE VOICE (nar-uh-tiv voy-se) The voice in the <u>story</u> that speaks to the reader. This is not always the <u>author</u>'s voice. The author can adopt another persona (i.e. pretend to be someone else).

NARRATOR (na-ray-tor) The voice telling the <u>story</u>, reciting the <u>narrative</u>. The narrator can be in the story themselves or they can be telling the story about someone else.

NEGATIVE PREFIX A group of <u>letters</u> which when added to a <u>word</u>, give the opposite meaning to the word.

<u>word</u>	<u>negative prefix</u>
obedient	*dis*obedient
understanding	*mis*understanding
climax	*anti*climax

NEOLOGISM (ne-ol-odg-is-am) A <u>word</u>, term or <u>phrase</u> that has been created recently to apply to new ideas or concepts. Neologisms are particularly useful in identifying new inventions or old ideas that have taken on a new cultural context, e.g. *email, blog, blackhole, pro-life, chav, pooper scooper.*

NEWSLETTER A <u>letter</u> written to convey information to a particular <u>audience</u>, e.g. a *school newsletter* has an audience of parents and students.

Newsletters are written in <u>Standard English</u> and tend to report events that have happened and list upcoming events and special dates.

NEWSPAPER is produced daily or weekly and contains information, news, opinion, <u>article</u>s and competitions aimed at a general <u>audience</u>.

The writers (<u>journalists</u>) tend to use either <u>Broadsheet writing</u> or <u>Tabloid writing</u>.

NON-FICTION (non-fick-shun) is <u>writing</u> about real life things or events, e.g. in *newspapers, magazines, encyclopaedias* or *instructions*.

NONSENSE POEMS do not make any real sense. They are entertaining, written for fun and are funny by being silly. Nonsense poems often <u>rhyme</u> and have a catchy <u>rhythm</u>.

'The Jabberwocky'

'Twas brillig, and the slithy toves
Did gyre and gimble in the wabe:
All mimsy were the borogoves,
And the mome raths outgrabe.

'Beware the Jabberwock, my son!
The jaws that bite, the claws that catch!
Beware the Jubjub bird and shun
The frumious Bandersnatch!'

He took his vorpal sword in hand:
Long time the manxome foe he sought –
So rested he by the Tumtum tree
And stood awhile in thought.

And, as in uffish thought he stood,
The Jabberwock, with eyes of flame,
Came whiffling through the tulgey wood,
And burbled as it came!

One, two! One, two! And through and through
The vorpal blade went snicker-snack!
He left it dead, and with its head
He went galumphing back.

'And hast thou slain the Jabberwock?
Come to my arms, my beamish boy!
O frabjous day! Callooh! Callay!'
He chortled in his joy.

'Twas brillig, and the slithy toves
Did gyre and gimble in the wabe:
All mimsy were the borogoves,
And the mome raths outgrabe.

by Lewis Carroll

NON-STANDARD ENGLISH (Also known as Slang.) Words and phrases which are often used in everyday speech but they are generally not considered to be part of Standard English.

We may say things differently from the ways in which we would write them. Non-standard English may differ from standard English in two ways:

♦   **grammar** – the way we form sentences

He ain't done nothing.
is a way of trying to say he hasn't done anything, but the double negative makes it mean that he actually has done something.

♦ **vocabulary** – the words that are used

cool ⟹	great
wicked ⟹	good
quid ⟹	pounds sterling
to kick the bucket ⟹	to die
to nick or *to knock off* ⟹	to steal

These expressions are often funny but should not be used in formal writing or formal speech.

NOTA BENE (N.B.) (noter-ben-ay) A Latin phrase meaning "Note Well". In modern English it means to "pay attention" or "take notice". It is used to draw the attention of the reader to a certain aspect or detail in the subject matter. It is often written as the abbreviation N.B.

NOTES The making of a brief summary of the key information in a piece of text. Students write down key words, phrases or terms which they identify as important. Notes can be brief and act as an aide mémoire that make sense to the writer but might not be understood by someone else.

NOUN (nown) is a naming word. A noun is the name of a person, place, animal or thing. Every thing and every person has a name and that name is a noun. They are one of the nine parts of speech.

● ***Common*** (or ordinary) nouns describe general things or people. They are called "common" nouns because the name is common to all persons or things of the same kind. Common nouns can usually have the words 'the', 'a' or 'an' put in front of them. Common nouns begin with a lower case letter.

people	places	things
baker	village	table
policeman	town	ruler
plumber	country	pen

- **Proper** nouns are the names of particular people, places or things. Proper nouns begin with capital letters (upper case).

people	places	things
John	Harrow	Monday
Doug	Cornwall	November
Elizabeth	England	The Guinness Book of Records

- **Collective** nouns (sometimes known as group terms) are the names for special groups of people, animals or things. Collective nouns are usually singular and have no capital letters.

people	animals	things
A *team* of players	A *flock* of birds	A *forest* of trees
A *choir* of singers	A *litter* of puppies	A *suit* of clothes
A *crowd* of spectators	A *pack* of wolves	A *pack* of cards

- **Abstract** nouns represent thoughts, ideas and feelings. They are names given to emotions and ideas. You cannot touch, taste, smell, hear or see these things.

idea, wonder, wisdom, anger, hope, sympathy, jealousy

- **Concrete** nouns are names of things you can actually touch, smell, hear, see and taste. They are things which exists outside your mind.

  keyboard, sugar, picture, music, perfume

- **Singular** nouns are just one thing, e.g. *a wave, an apple, the game, one toe.* (Also see Singular.)

- **Plural** nouns mean more than one. (Also see Plural.) A <u>singular</u> noun can be made into a plural noun in the following ways.

add 's'	nouns ending in 'f' or 'fe' use 'ves'	nouns ending in 'o', 'x' or 'ch' add 'es'
waves	knives	potatoes
games	thieves	boxes
toes	wives	beaches

- **Noun Phrases** act as nouns in <u>sentences</u>. They do all the things that nouns can do. (Also see Phrases.)

  All the people in the crowd began to cheer as he arrived.

NOVEL A long <u>story</u>, divided into <u>chapters</u> that takes up a whole <u>book</u>. A book with just one story and which usually does not contain any pictures. In terms of length, a novel would be considered to be a work of <u>literature</u> of 50,000 words or more.

NOVELLA A piece of <u>writing</u> that is longer than a <u>short story</u> but shorter than a <u>novel</u>. In terms of length, a novella would be considered to be in the region of 20,000-50,000 words.

  'A Christmas Carol' by Charles Dickens

  'Of Mice and Men' by John Steinbeck

NURSERY RHYME is a <u>poem</u> or <u>song</u> learnt by young children. They tell a simple <u>story</u> in a <u>rhyme</u> that is easy to learn, remember and recite.

> *Jack and Jill went up the hill*
> *To fetch a pail of water*
> *Jack fell down and broke his crown*
> *And Jill came tumbling after*
>
> Anon.

OBITUARY (oh-bich-oo-er-ee) An account, written after a person has died, which provides the reader with a summary of the person's life. Obituaries are usually about someone famous and are written in <u>newspaper</u>s or <u>magazine</u>s often by someone who knew them personally or was well acquainted with their life.

Sometimes obituaries are written before the person's death and saved. They are then updated and published after the subject has died.

OBJECT is found in some <u>sentence</u>s and usually comes after the <u>verb</u>.

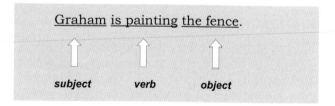

ODE (ohd) A <u>poem</u> devoted to the praise of a person, animal or thing. An ode is usually written in a way that expresses deep feeling, enthusiastic emotion and dignity of style.

In classical times, an ode was a poem intended to be sung.

> *'Ode to a Nightingale'* by John Keates

ONOMATOPOEIA (on-oh-mat-oh-pee-yah) is the use of <u>words</u> that sound like what they mean.

> The bees were *buzzing.*
>
> The leaves *rustled.*
>
> The fire *crackled.*

OPPOSITE (See Antonym.)

ORACY (oh-ra-see) Oral communication and <u>comprehension</u>. The ability both to convey thoughts and ideas orally in a way that others understand, and to understand what others say.

ORATION (oh-ra-shun) A formal speech which may be given in a ceremonial setting.

A speech that may be considered pompous, boring or inappropriately long.

An academic speech often given as an exercise in public speaking and that is designed to show the speaker's <u>rhetoric</u>al skills.

ORAL TRADITION (or-al tra-dish-shun) The cultural and historical background of a community that is preserved and passed on from generation to generation in spoken <u>stories</u> and <u>songs</u>, as distinct from being written down.

ORTHOGRAPHY (or-th-og-raf-ee) considers the use of <u>letters</u> and the ways they are combined into <u>words</u>. It is also the study of correct spellings according to the accepted, conventional usage in a <u>language</u>.

OVERVIEW is a short summary that provides the reader with information about the main points and ideas or <u>themes</u> of a <u>text</u>.

OVERWORKED WORD A <u>word</u> that tends to be used too much so that its meaning becomes vague and imprecise, e.g. *nice, amazing, good, fine.*

When used in the correct places their meanings can be understood but particularly in <u>writing</u>, alternative words will often sound better and be more descriptive, e.g. *beautiful, delicious, effective.*

OXYMORON (oxee-mor-on) A <u>figure of speech</u> that includes two normally contradictory terms. They are used intentionally in <u>writing</u> for <u>rhetorical</u> effect. By combining two terms, a novel expression of some concept can be created.

> Some popular oxymoron:
>
> *Bitter sweet*   *Cruel to be kind*
> *Pretty ugly*   *Random order*
> *Expect the unexpected*   *Deafening silence*

William Shakespeare used oxymoron for Juliet's speech when she discovered that Romeo had killed her cousin, Tybalt.

> *O serpent heart, hid with a flow'ring face!*
> *Beautiful tyrant, fiend angelical*
> *Dove-feathered raven, wolfish ravening lamb*
> *A damned saint, an honourable villain*

PAGINATION (paj-in-nay-shun) The figures, usually numbers, shown on the pages or leaves of a <u>book</u> to indicate the sequence of the pages.

PALINDROME A <u>word</u> that reads the same when read forwards or backwards, e.g. *madam, radar, noon, Abba, bib, solos, Hannah.*

PANGRAM A term for a <u>sentence</u> which uses every letter of the <u>alphabet</u> at least once.

> *The quick brown fox jumps over the lazy dog.*
>
> *My faxed joke won a pager in the cable TV quiz show.*

PANTOMIME (pan-toh-myme) Traditionally, the telling of a <u>story</u> without using words but by means of bodily movements, gestures and facial expressions.

Nowadays pantomime is a very English type of funny <u>play</u> which can be dramatic and spectacular. It may involve <u>dialogue</u>, music, singing and dancing with a <u>plot</u> loosely based on a familiar <u>traditional tale</u>, e.g. *Little Red Riding Hood, Cinderella, Jack and the Beanstalk* or *Dick Whittington*.

Pantomime is characterised by the lead male <u>role</u> played by a young woman known as the Principal Boy and includes at least one masculine man playing a woman (known as the pantomime dame). Popular as family entertainment, pantomimes are usually performed during the winter in the United Kingdom.

PARABLE (par-uh-buhl) A short descriptive <u>story</u> that illustrates a moral attitude or religious idea.

> In the *'Holy Bible'*, the Gospel of Matthew chapter 13 contains 6 parables.
>
> *Matthew 13:33*
>
> *"The kingdom of heaven is like yeast that a woman took and mixed into a large amount of flour until it worked all through the dough."*

PARADOX (pah-ro-dox) A <u>statement</u> that seems at first to be contrary to common sense but on reflection can provoke a fresh thought.

> 'A Tale of Two Cities' by Charles Dickens begins with the paradoxical statement "*It was the best of times, it was the worst of times.*"
>
> "*I always lie*" is a paradox because if it is true it must be false.
>
> "*This page has been left intentionally blank*". When this statement appears on an exam paper it is paradoxical.

PARAGRAPH (para-graf) A paragraph helps to break up chunks of <u>writing</u> into pieces that are easier to read and understand.   A new paragraph is <u>indent</u>ed slightly from the <u>margin</u> or a line space is missed out. Paragraphs should change when:

- ◆ a new person is introduced into the <u>story</u>
- ◆ a new place is introduced into the story
- ◆ there is a change of time
- ◆ a new speaker joins a conversation
- ◆ the writing is about a different time
- ◆ to show that something really important has happened

PARAPHRASE (para-fray-ze) To take a piece of <u>text</u> and reword or rewrite it without losing the original meaning, i.e. to express something in another way.

PARENTHESES (pah-ren-the-sees) (See the singular Parenthesis below.)

PARENTHESIS (pah-ren-the-sis) Either of the curved-<u>bracket</u> () <u>punctuation</u> marks that together make a set of <u>parentheses</u>.

It can also refer to the <u>word</u>, <u>clause</u> or <u>sentence</u> inside a pair of <u>brackets</u>, <u>dashes</u> or <u>commas</u>.

PARODY (pah-ro-dee) Imitating a <u>text</u> to make fun of it. Parody is not a direct copy of a text but it exaggerates it to cause an amusing effect with the aim of making people laugh. This is at the expense of the original text which is made to look ridiculous.

PARSING The process of identifying the component <u>words</u> in a <u>sentence</u> and describing their <u>parts of speech</u> and their relation to other words in the sentence.

PARTS OF SPEECH The jobs that different types of words do in <u>sentences</u>. There are nine of these: <u>Noun</u>, <u>Pronoun</u>, <u>Verb</u>, <u>Adjective</u>, <u>Adverb</u>, <u>Preposition</u>, <u>Conjunction/ Connective</u>, <u>Interjection</u>, <u>Article</u>.

PASSIVE VERB (pas-iv verb) (See Verb.)

PASSIVE VOICE (pas-iv voy-se) The "voice" of the <u>verb</u> which shows that the <u>subject</u> is having the action done to it.

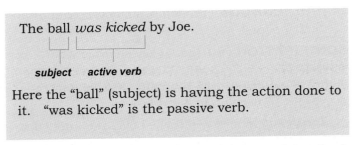

The ball *was kicked* by Joe.

subject   **active verb**

Here the "ball" (subject) is having the action done to it. "was kicked" is the passive verb.

The passive voice can give a particular kind of emphasis to <u>sentences</u>. Public notices are often written in the passive voice because it is less aggressive and abrupt than the <u>active voice</u>. (Also see Verb, Active and Passive.)

PAST PARTICIPLE (parst pah-tis-i-pul) The part of a <u>verb</u> that follows "has" or "have" in the <u>past tense</u>.

> I *have eaten.*
>
> I *have run.*

PAST PERFECT TENSE (Also see Conjugation.) A tense used to express an action completed in past time, e.g. *I had walked.*

PAST TENSE (Also see Conjugation.) A verb tense used to express actions that occurred in or during the past, e.g. *I walked.*

PATHOS (pay-thos) In <u>literature</u>, the quality of <u>writing</u> and expression that arouses in the reader or <u>audience</u> feelings of pity, sympathy, tenderness or sorrow.

PEN NAME (Also see Pseudonym.) A name used by a writer instead of his/her real name.

> Mary Anne Evans used the name *'George Elliot'.*
>
> Charles Dodgson used the name *'Lewis Carroll'.*

PERSONAL PRONOUN (per-son-al pro-nown) (See Pronoun.)

PERSONIFICATION (per-son-ify-kay-shun) is where an object without life (like the sea or the sky) is given human or animal qualities such as thoughts and feelings.

> The *threatening* sky darkened over the *angry* sea.
>
> The lonely tree *shivered* and *moaned* in the freezing wind.

PERSUASIVE WRITING (per-sway-siv ri-ting) A <u>style of writing</u> that aims to make one particular <u>point of view</u> more acceptable than another. It involves writing in a way that is positive and certain, using <u>exaggeration</u>, <u>rhetorical questions</u> and evidence, to back up points that are made.

PHONETICS (fon-et-icks) A system of <u>spelling words</u> by representing <u>letters</u> by their sounds.

PHRASE (fray-ze) A group of two or more grammatically linked <u>words</u> which forms part of a <u>sentence</u>. A phrase functions as a single unit in the <u>syntax</u> of the sentence but does not make sense on its own. A phrase does not contain a <u>subject</u> or <u>predicate</u> and so is distinguished from a <u>clause</u>.

A phrase can replace one word and help to make sentences longer and more interesting. Various types of phrases can be identified.

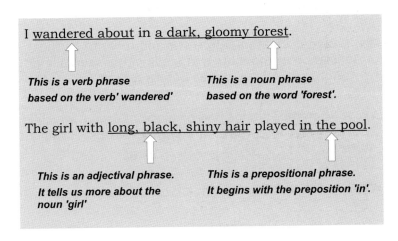

I <u>wandered about</u> in <u>a dark, gloomy forest</u>.

This is a verb phrase
based on the verb' wandered'

This is a noun phrase
based on the word 'forest'.

The girl with <u>long, black, shiny hair</u> played <u>in the pool</u>.

This is an adjectival phrase.
It tells us more about the noun 'girl'

This is a prepositional phrase.
It begins with the preposition 'in'.

Adverbial phrases can be used to tell how, when or where an action is done.

Adverbial phrase	type
She played *with great skill.*	how
She returned *very early in the morning.*	when
The car skidded *into the tree.*	where

In general use a phrase refers to any frequently repeated or memorable group of words which have widely recognised meaning when used in the correct context.

local derby	*a walk on the wild side*
not to be sneezed at	*to coin a phrase*
hedge your bets	*pulling my leg*

PLAN A plan is created before starting to write by the organisation of thoughts and ideas either mentally or in written form. A plan comes before a draft.

PLAY A dramatic composition or piece of drama which is written with the purpose of being performed (usually on a stage).

PLAY ON WORDS (See Pun.)

PLAYSCRIPT A play written as a script which is then acted out. Playscripts have instructions on how the play is to be performed. These are known as the stage directions. These include scenes, what the actors say and how they say it and what is happening on stage. Speech shown in a playscript does not have inverted commas or speech marks.

PLOT The main events that take place in a <u>novel</u>, <u>story</u>, film or <u>play</u>. A summary of the main outline with little description or elaboration.

PLOTLINE (See Storyline.)

PLOT TWIST (See Twist in the Tale.)

PLURAL (ploo-ral) A <u>word</u> which refers to more than one thing. When <u>singular</u> words become plural they usually change their <u>spelling</u> slightly to show the difference in their meaning. The way they change usually depends on what letter they end with in the singular.

◆ For most plurals add an '*s*' to the singular:

singular	plural
table	tables
chair	chairs
computer	computers

◆ For words ending in *ch*, *sh*, *ss*, *x* (hissing sounds), add '*es*':

singular	plural
box	boxes
dress	dresses
match	matches

- For words where there is a <u>vowel</u> before the '*y*', so ending in *ay, ey, oy*, add '*s*':

singular	plural
day	days
key	keys
chimney	chimneys

- For other words ending in '*y*' and where there is a <u>consonant</u> before the '*y*', change the '*y*' to '*ies*':

singular	plural
baby	babies
city	cities
country	countries

- For some words ending in '*f* ' add '*s*':

singular	plural
proof	proofs
chief	chiefs
belief	beliefs

- For most words ending in '*f* ' change the '*f* ' to '*ves*':

singular	plural
half	halves
leaf	leaves
thief	thieves

- For words ending in '*o*' add '*es*':

singular	plural
volcano	volcanoes
tomato	tomatoes
potato	potatoes

- Exceptions to the above rule:

singular	plural
piano	pianos
solo	solos

- Some words remain the same in both singular and plural:

singular	plural
sheep	sheep
deer	deer
scissors	scissors
trousers	trousers
salmon	salmon
aircraft	aircraft

- In some words only the <u>vowel</u> changes:

singular	plural
man	men
foot	feet
tooth	teeth

• Exceptions:

singular	plural
mouse	mice

PLURAL NOUN (ploo-ral nown) (See Noun.)

PLURAL PRONOUN (ploo-ral pro-nown) (See Pronoun.)

POEM (poh-em) A literary composition written in blank verse or in rhyme characterised by the use of language which is imaginative, chosen for its sound, suggestive power and beauty and uses poetical techniques such as metre, metaphor and rhyme.

Examples of types of poems include: acrostic, ballad, calligram, cinquain, clerihew, concrete, elegy, haiku, lament, limerick, lyric, narrative, nonsense, ode, renga, shape, sonnet, tanka.

POET A person who composes and writes poetry.

POETIC DEVICE (po-et-ick de-vi-se) The way that words, sounds and phrases are arranged in poems to create emotion, imagery, rhythm and rhyme. An awareness of poetic devices can help you understand better the ways that poems can be written and assist your understanding of them.

Some of the more common poetic devices are: alliteration, allusion, analogy, assonance, diction, echo, enjambment, hyperbole, imagery, metaphor, metonym, metre, mood, onomatopoeia, oxymoron, paradox, repetition, rhythm, rhyme, rhyming couplets, rhyme scheme, personification, point of view, simile, symbol, tone.

POETIC FORM (po-et-ick for-m) The arrangement chosen by the poet to convey the content of the poem setting out the *way* that the poem is said rather than what it contains or *what* is said.

The way that the poem has been composed can be compared to the conventional poetic structures such as ballads, haiku, cinquain, etc. in order to highlight both similarities and differences with established poetic arrangements.

POETIC JUSTICE (po-et-ick just-iss) An outcome, found in literature in which characters are rewarded and bad characters punished. When a writer deploys this technique effectively is when one character seeks to bring down another but ends up being caught in their own trap.

POETIC LICENCE (po-et-ick li-sense) (See Artistic Licence.)

POETIC STYLE (po-et-ick st-ile) The way a poem is written, considering the words chosen, the kinds of pictures painted by those words, the use of rhythm and the lengths of lines. Poetic style is not so much about what is written but the way it is written.

POETRY (po-et-ree) A division of literature represented by the work of a poet. Poetry is characterised by rhythmical composition which may be written or spoken with the purpose of giving pleasure, by the expression in words of beautiful, imaginative or elevated thoughts. The art of the poem.

POETRY ANALYSIS (po-et-ree an-al-eh-sis) A process used to find out more about a <u>poem</u>. It might feature as part of an examination task or question. A poetry analysis might include <u>commentary</u> on:

- Introduction – the <u>title</u> of the poem and name of the <u>poet</u>. <u>Poetry</u> type, e.g. *sonnet, haiku*, etc.

- Subject of the poem.

- <u>Theme</u>s of the poem – what is the poem about? Is there a <u>story</u> the poem tells?

- <u>Imagery</u> used to express <u>themes</u> – what pictures are created by the poem? Are <u>metaphors</u>, <u>similies</u> and <u>personification</u> used?

- <u>Poetic form</u> and <u>structure</u> – poem organisation, <u>comment</u> on lines, <u>verses</u>, <u>layout</u> and shape. Why has the <u>poet</u> structured ideas in the way chosen? How has it helped communicate ideas?

- <u>Rhyme scheme</u> and <u>rhythm</u> – how does the poem <u>rhyme</u>, e.g. *AABB, ABAB*. When the poem is read aloud, what is the rhythm? Why has this rhyme and rhythm been chosen?

- <u>Language</u> patterns – is the sound of the poem and the choice of words interesting? Is there use of <u>alliteration</u>, <u>onomatopoeia</u>, <u>assonance</u>, <u>personification</u> or <u>symbolism</u>?

- Poet's message – what is the poet trying to say to the reader? How effective are the <u>poetic devices</u> and language used? What is the reader's response to the poem?

POINT OF VIEW The way the <u>story</u> or incidents in the story are looked at by the <u>narrator</u>. The point of view provided by the narrator is the view through which the reader experiences the story. If, for example, a child is observing and commenting on the actions of adults, the point of view adopted will be based on how the child feels about the adult's behaviour.

In the <u>first person</u> point of view, the narrator is a participant in the story. In the <u>third person</u> point of view, the story is told by a narrator who is not one of the story's participants.

PORTRAIT (por-trayt) Used in the <u>layout</u> or framing of <u>text</u> or pictures, where the vertical height of the frame is longer than the horizontal width of the frame. It is derived from the vertical rectangular layout of a traditional classical portrait painting. The opposite layout is known as <u>landscape</u>.

POSSESIVE PRONOUN (po-zes-iv pro-nown) (See Pronoun.)

POSTER A way of communicating information in a highly visual way. Posters are eye-catching sheets of paper or card that are wall mounted. They can be used for advertisements or to give information. Effective posters will have:

- picture illustrations or simple diagrams

- a <u>title</u> or <u>headline</u>

- bright contrasting colours or be black and white

- important details, e.g. a poster advertising a concert or event would include the date, starting times and price, often <u>highlight</u>ed or shown in bold

PRACTICAL LESSON (See Moral Lesson.)

PRÉCIS (pray-see) To summarise a lot of information into a more brief but factually accurate account.

PREDICATE (pred-ee-kate) The part of a <u>sentence</u> that says most about the <u>subject</u> or thing the sentence is about. The predicate always includes the <u>verb</u> of the sentence.

Graham *is painting the fence.*

PREFIX (pree-fix) <u>Letters</u> that are added to the beginnings of <u>word</u>s to change the meaning or for use in word building.

> happy ⟹ *un*happy
>
> lock ⟹ *un*lock

PREPOSITION (prep-o-zi-shun) A <u>word</u> which shows where one thing is in relation to another, or the "position" that it is in. Prepositions help connect two <u>nouns</u> or <u>pronouns</u> in a <u>sentence</u>.

> The clock is *on* the wall.
>
> The computer is *in* the corner.
>
> My feet are *under* the table.

Prepositions can also be made up of groups of words.

> The dog ran *out of* the house.
>
> They had all been good *except for* Don.

PREPOSITIONAL PHRASE (See Phrase.)

PRESENT PARTICIPLE (prez-ent par-tis-i-pul) A part of a <u>verb</u> that usually ends with the <u>suffix</u> '*ing*', e.g. scor*ing*, cheer*ing*, help*ing*.

PRESENT PERFECT TENSE (Also see Conjugation.) The verb tense used to express action completed in the present time, e.g. *I have walked.*

PRESENT TENSE (prez-ent ten-se) (Also see Conjugation.) The verb tense expressing action in the present time, e.g. *I walk.*

PRIMARY WORD (See Root Word.)

PROLOGUE (pro-log) An introduction to the main <u>text</u>. Originally used in Greek <u>drama</u>, prologues are found in Shakespeare <u>plays</u>, long <u>poems</u> and some <u>novels</u>.

PRONOUN (pro-nown) A pronoun stands in the place of a <u>noun</u>. It is useful as it helps a <u>sentence</u> to flow more smoothly and avoids having to repeat the same <u>word</u> again and again. Pronouns are short words and the main ones are: *I, you, he, she, it, we, they, me, him, her, them*.

- **Personal** pronouns can be used as the <u>subject</u> of a sentence, e.g. *I, you, they, we, it, she, he*.

> *I* looked at Graham when *he* scored the goal.

Personal pronouns can also be used as the <u>object</u> of a sentence, e.g. *them, us, it, her, him, you, me*.

> I looked at *her* as she poked *him*.

Sometimes it is difficult to decide whether to use '*me*' or '*I* '. If it is part of the <u>predicate</u>, use '*me*'. The rule is to put yourself last when writing about yourself and someone else.

> The Queen may say:
> *"My husband and I ..."*

To check, remove the other person or thing from the <u>sentence</u> and see if it still makes sense.

> *Me and my family went to the zoo.*
> Remove '*and my family*' and it reads
> *Me went to the zoo.*   (this is incorrect)
>
> It should be:
> *My family and I went to the zoo.*
> Remove '*My family and*' and it reads:
> *I went to the zoo.*   (this is correct)

- **Possessive** pronouns are used in place of nouns that show possession. Such nouns always have an apostrophe but don't when replaced by a possessive pronoun.

> Is that Connor's football?
>
> becomes:
>
> Is that *his* football?

These are possessive pronouns: *mine, yours, his, her, its, ours, yours, theirs.*

- **Singular** pronouns are <u>singular</u> (one person or thing), e.g. *I, he, you, me, she, it, him, her.*

- **Plural** pronouns are <u>plural</u> (more than one person or thing), e.g. *they, us, them, you. 'You'* can be used for both singular and plural.

- **Reflexive** pronouns (Also known as Compound Pronouns.) Sometimes personal pronouns are turned into reflexive pronouns by adding 'self' or 'selves', e.g. *himself, itself, herself, yourself, themselves, ourselves.* These are known as reflexive pronouns because they **reflect** back to an earlier noun or pronoun.

- **Interrogative** pronouns stand in for nouns in <u>question</u>s, e.g. *who, whom, whose, which, what.* These pronouns help to ask questions or interrogate.

- **Indefinite** pronouns take the place of unspecified persons, places or things, e.g. *none, any, other, some, each, either, neither, few, several.*

- **Relative** pronouns help to connect or relate one part of a sentence to another, e.g. *who, whom, whose, which, that, what.*

- **Demonstrative** pronouns point out a person or thing specifically, e.g. *this, that, these, those.*

PRONUNCIATION (pro-nun-see-ay-shun) The way that <u>words</u> sound when they are spoken. The ways that <u>syllables</u> and <u>letters</u> within words are stressed to produce word sounds.

PROOF A version of a <u>manuscript</u> that has been typeset and is the final trial print used for checking and to make corrections before the final printing.

PROOFREADING The reading of a <u>proof</u> copy of a <u>text</u> in order to detect and correct any errors like extra spaces, <u>punctuation</u>, <u>spelling</u>, alignment, <u>font</u> type, <u>style</u> and other details.

PROPER NOUN (See Noun.)

PROSE (prohz) The ordinary, everyday form of spoken and written <u>language</u>. A type of <u>literature</u> which is different from <u>poetry</u> as it uses language which follows less regular patterns and includes a variety of <u>rhythm</u>.

PROSODY (pro-so-dee) considers the use of the manners of speaking and reading and particularly the patterns of stress and <u>intonation</u> in a <u>language</u>.

It is also the study of poetic <u>metre</u> and the different kinds of <u>verse</u>.

PROTAGONIST The main <u>character</u> in a <u>story</u>, <u>drama</u> or other work of <u>literature</u> with whom the reader or <u>audience</u> is meant to identify. Whilst the character may not necessarily be "good" by any conventional moral standard, they are the person whose plight and destiny is being followed with most interest.

> Hamlet is the protagonist in the play that bears his name and which was written by William Shakespeare.
>
> Prince Caspian is the protagonist in the story that bears his name and which was written by C.S.Lewis.

The counterpart to the protagonist in a work of <u>literature</u> is a character known as the <u>antagonist</u>.

PROVERB A well known saying expressed in a clever and brief manner. They have a real or literal meaning but also contain a message of real wisdom.

> You've managed to buy that new CD. When I went, all the shops had sold out.
>
> (Proverb: *The early bird catches the worm*)

PSEUDONYM (seu-doh-nim) (Also see Pen Name.) A false name, one that is not somebody's original name. Especially used by <u>actors</u> or <u>authors</u> not wanting to reveal their real name.

PULP FICTION <u>Novels</u> written for the mass market, intended for "easy-reading" or to be a "good read". Such novels are often exciting, titillating and thrilling.

PUN (Also known as a Play on Words.) A <u>figure of speech</u> made up of a <u>word</u> or a <u>sentence</u> which sounds the same but which has two meanings. Often this play on words produces an amusing result.

> Cinderella left, leaving the *ball* behind.
> Has Cinderella been playing football or has she had to leave the dance?
>
> "*Aisle, altar, hymn*", whispered the bride as she remembered the order of her wedding service.
>
> This could simply be the bride reminding herself of the order of the wedding service or it sounds like and could mean "I'll alter him" referring to her intention towards her new husband.

PUNCTUATION (punk-tyoo-ay-shun) is the use of punctuation marks.

PUNCTUATION MARK (punk-tyoo-ay-shun mark) A mark used to help our <u>writing</u> make sense and be understood by a reader.   Punctuation marks can be divided into:

- ◆ *long stops* are used to end <u>sentences</u>.

> .   a full stop also called a period
>
> ?   a question mark
>
> !   an exclamation mark

- ◆ *short stops* which are used within sentences to make the sense clearer.

> ,   comma   ( )   brackets
>
> -   hyphen   :   colon
>
> —   dashes   ;   semi-colon

Punctuation marks include the correct use of <u>capital letters</u> and <u>quotation marks</u>.

QUESTION (kwes-chun) A <u>sentence</u> which requires an answer, e.g. *Are you cold?* These sentences end with a <u>question mark</u>. (Also see <u>direct question</u> and <u>indirect question</u>.)

Sometimes just one word is a question by itself and this too needs to be followed by a question mark.

> *How?*   *Why?*
>
> *Where?*   *What?*
>
> *When?*   *Who?*

QUESTION MARK (kwes-chun mark) A <u>punctuation mark</u> (?) used at the end of a <u>sentence</u> which asks a <u>question</u>. It carries its own <u>full stop</u> so the next <u>word</u> begins with a <u>capital letter</u>.

QUESTION TAG (kwes-chun tag) A grammatical structure in which a <u>statement</u>, <u>imperative</u> or <u>command sentence</u> is turned into a <u>question</u> by adding an interrogative ending (the question tag).

> I was right, *wasn't I?*
>
> He is the best tutor, *isn't he?*
>
> Open the window, *will you?*

QUOTATION (kwo-tay-shun) Repeating the exact <u>words</u> that someone has spoken. The exact words copied from a <u>book</u>, <u>magazine</u> or <u>newspaper</u>. When written down, an <u>extract</u> should be enclosed in <u>quotation marks</u>.

QUOTATION MARK (kwo-tay-shun mark) <u>Punctuation marks</u> (" ") that are used to show the exact <u>words</u> someone has spoken. The marks enclose the <u>quotation</u>, sometimes referred to as 'quotes'.

RAP POEM has a distinctive <u>rhythm</u> and a beat or <u>metre</u> which gives a regular pattern of stressed and unstressed <u>syllables</u>. Rap <u>poems</u> can be read as a chant and with clapping or drumming to add effect to the stressed syllables. Rap poems often tell a <u>story</u> like a <u>ballad</u>.

The Tutor Master Rap:

Going to Tutor Master on a Tuesday night
Hoping that I'm gonna get my sums all right.
He teaches me so well,
He's such a nice chap.
Everybody clap and do the Tutor Master rap.

Tutor Master, Tutor Master you're so cool.
You make sure we keep the golden rule.
Mark with a red pen,
Tick, tick, tick.
Be a quicker sticker picker, stick, stick, stick.

If I work hard and do my best
He'll help me pass every test.
Add those sums,
Get ten out of ten,
Then do the super Tutor Master rap once again.

RECEIVED PRONUNCIATION (ree-seeved pro-nun-see-ay-shun) What most people would agree is the correct way to pronounce good English. Dictionaries show how words are normally spoken using phonetics, in brackets, after the word is listed but before the definition.

Whilst pronunciation can vary from one part of a country to another, national radio and television have helped to establish received pronunciation as a common standard.

REFLEXIVE PRONOUN (re-flex-iv pro-nown) (See Pronoun.)

RELATIVE PRONOUN (rel-a-tiv pro-nown) (See Pronoun.)

RENGA (reng-ga) A series of haiku written in sequence by different people on a similar subject.

REPETITION (rep-er-ti-shun) The repeating of the same <u>words</u> or <u>phrases</u> can be unnecessary and this can make <u>writing</u> seem boring for the reader. When writing <u>direct speech</u>, instead of writing 'said', the writer could use 'replied', 'asked', 'muttered', 'whispered', <u>etc</u>. as alternatives to the word 'said', to make the <u>text</u> more varied.

In <u>poems</u> and <u>prose</u>, the use of repetition, however, can be deliberate. Constantly repeating the same word is a <u>device</u> that can be used effectively to add interest.

> In the poem 'Morning Rush', the word 'quickly' is repeated to give a special effect:
>
> *Quickly* the commuter hurries down the street
>
> *Quickly* the patter of school bound feet
>
> *Quickly* the cars dash away from the lights
>
> *Quickly* the cyclists pedal their bikes
>
> *Quickly* the train carries city bound workers
>
> And *quickly* goes time for the late to school shirkers.

REPORT A piece of <u>formal writing</u> giving detailed information relating to a particular <u>question</u> or <u>hypothesis</u>. Reports include both facts and opinions and consider both the advantages and disadvantages of the points raised by the question. The <u>layout</u> of reports is in <u>paragraphs</u> with major points given <u>subheadings</u> to help the reader.

REPORTED SPEECH (Also known as Indirect Speech.) Where we do not use the exact <u>words</u> spoken by someone but we report what they said in our own words. <u>Speech marks</u> are not used for reported speech.

> *"I enjoy going to football", said Paul.*
>
> In reported speech this would be written:
>
> *Paul said that he enjoyed going to football.*

RESOLUTION (Also known as Denouement.) The part of a story structure that follows the climax and falling action. It is used in literature to describe the series of events that follow the plot's climax and provides a conclusion or resolution of the intricacies of the story.

RETRONYM (ret-ro-nim) A name for a word, term or phrase which has been created recently when the original name has come to be used for something else or is no longer unique.

> *World War One* was originally called The Great War.
>
> *Hard Copy* is used instead of Paper Copy.
>
> *Fin Fish* is used to distinguish real fish from shell fish.

REVIEWS (re-vu-s) are written about plays and stories to tell the reader what they are about and what they are like. A review comments on the themes and presentation of the play or story. It gives some information about the play or story and the reviewer's impression, opinion and comments about what the whole piece was like.

RHETORIC (ret-or-ic) Using speech or writing in a way that is meant to persuade or impress. This may involve language that is extravagant, exaggerated or insincere in order to convince.

RHETORICAL DEVICE (ret-or-i-cal de-vi-se) A technique used to argue or persuade. These include rhetorical questions, metaphors, similes, exaggeration, alliteration, etc.

One device is known as a 'group of three', where three items are placed together.

> You may all vote for us, *the good, the bad and the ugly.*
>
> Our policies have been *seen, tried and tested.*
>
> Our priorities are *education, education, education.*

RHETORICAL QUESTION (ret-or-i-cal kwes-chun) (See Rhetorical Device.) A <u>question</u> that does not require a straight 'yes' or 'no' answer but is used to make you think, or to make you do something.

> *How many times have I told you not to do that?*
>
> *Don't you think it's time to get up?*
>
> *Who cares?*

RHYME (rime) <u>Word</u>s whose endings sound the same. When two words end with a similar sound they rhyme with each other. In <u>poetry</u> the words that rhyme are often found at the end of a line. In some poetry, the pattern of the rhymes is the same in each <u>verse</u>.

A rhyme can also be a <u>poem</u> or verse composed in such a way that words or <u>syllable</u>s with similar sounds are repeated between two or more lines. The <u>repetition</u> of sounds is usually at the end of the lines as in <u>rhyming couplet</u>s but it can also be in <u>internal rhyme</u> as in the following <u>nursery rhyme</u>.

> *Cuckoo, cuckoo, what do you do?*
> *In April I open my bill;*
> *In May I sing all the day;*
> *In June I change my tune;*
> *In July away I fly;*
> *In August away I must.*
> (Anon.)

RHYME PATTERN (rime pat-turn) (See Rhyme Scheme.)

RHYME SCHEME (rime skeem) (Also known as Rhyme Pattern.) How a <u>poem</u> is structured and which lines <u>rhyme</u> together. The rhyme scheme is often shown as <u>letters</u>, e.g. *A-A-B-B* in a <u>clerihew</u> where the first and second lines rhyme together and the last two lines rhyme together.

Sir Donald Ross	A
Said, "I'm feeling quite cross."	A
My team lose every game	B
It seems such a shame!	B

RHYMING COUPLET (rime-ing cup-let) Occurs in <u>poems</u> where the first two lines <u>rhyme</u> together and the second two lines rhyme together and have the same <u>metre</u>.

Tutor master is so cool
He helps me to succeed at school

RHYTHM (rith-um) A pattern of <u>syllables</u> used in poetry so that each line has a set number of syllables meaning that the <u>poem</u> can be read easily.

RIDDLE (rid-ell) A clever <u>question</u> that has been worded in a puzzling way.

"Which came first, the chicken or the egg?"

"I know a word of letters three. Add two and fewer there will be."
[Answer: the word *"few"*]

"What is it that when you take away the whole you still have some left over?"
[Answer: the word *"wholesome"*]

RISING ACTION The part of a story structure that follows the complication and sets out the events that occur within the story, prolonging and developing the central conflict.

ROLE (roll) A technique used in drama when people pretend to be someone else. To be effective in a role a person must try to be as much like the new character as possible, adopting the voice, facial expressions, body language and feelings of the character they are representing.

ROOT VERB (Also see Verb and Conjugation.) The verb before any changes have been made to account for the tense.

Root verb	Present tense	Past tense
walk	walking	walked
close	closing	closed
shout	shouting	shouted

ROOT WORD (Also known as a Primary Word.) A word in its simplest form, e.g. *bed, room, white, board.*

SARCASM (sar-kas-am) Where verbal irony is often accompanied by a tone of voice expressing sneering, scorning, contemptuous disapproval whilst pretending to sound like praise of a person or thing.

SATIRE A form of literature in which ridicule, sarcasm, irony, derision or wit is used to point out human folly or vice. Its use implies a moral judgement and its use and purpose is often corrective and usually intended to bring about a change in the behaviour ridiculed.

'1984', a novel by George Orwell, is a satire of totalitarian states. At the time he was writing these were the Soviet Union and Nazi Germany.

Another novel written by George Orwell, 'Animal Farm', is an allegorical satire of the Russian Revolution.

SCANNING Reading through a piece of <u>text</u> quickly in order to pick out or identify <u>key words</u> and <u>phrases</u> that will help your understanding of what the text is about. Scanning can also involve using pictures to help provide visual clues to assist <u>comprehension</u>.

SCENE (seen) A short piece of continuous action in a <u>play</u>. Scenes break up the main <u>story</u> and show where time has passed or where the story has moved to a different place. Several scenes can make up an <u>act</u>.

SCIENCE FICTION (si-ents fick-shun) Stories which can have a <u>theme</u> of space, time travel and aliens. They are often set:

- on the earth but in the future
- in another world or elsewhere in space
- in another world or elsewhere in space in the future

SCRIPT (sk-rip-t) could refer to:

- The <u>letters</u> or characters used in <u>writing</u> by hand, particularly <u>cursive</u> writing
- The <u>text</u> of a <u>manuscript</u> or <u>document</u>.
- The written text of a <u>play</u>, film, radio or television broadcast.

SECOND PERSON (sek-ond per-son) The grammatical category of <u>words</u> used to designate the person being spoken to. The 'person' used by a speaker in referring to the one or ones to whom she or he is speaking.

In English, 'you' is a second person <u>pronoun</u> which can be used as a form of address in both <u>singular</u> and <u>plural</u>.

It is also the <u>style of writing</u> used in which the <u>narrator</u> in the <u>story</u> recounts his or her experiences or impressions using the 'you' <u>point of view</u>.

Use of the second person is the least used of writing styles for stories. It is used more for writing of an instructional nature.

> If *you* want a good Tutor Master, consider going to www.tutormaster-services.co.uk.

SEMI-COLON (sem-ee ko-lon) A <u>punctuation mark</u> (;) which separates two groups of words which are closely linked in meaning. A semi-colon is a weaker punctuation mark than a <u>colon</u> but stronger than a <u>comma</u>.

> The team celebrated; they had just scored the winning goal.

Often the second half of the <u>sentence</u> (after the semi-colon) either tells us more about the first half, or tells us the result or cause of the first half.

It is important to realise that the two groups of words separated by the semi-colon must both be able to stand as sentences on their own.

> *Using the above example:*
>
> The team celebrated. They had just scored the winning goal.

Semi-colons are used to separate items in a list when commas are already being used.

In Dave's house there is a well-designed school room, containing books and a computer; a light and airy kitchen; a vast living room; several bathrooms; six bedrooms and an Olympic-sized swimming pool.

SENTENCE (sent-ens) A group of <u>words</u> which makes complete sense on its own. Sentences begin with a <u>capital letter</u> and end with a <u>full stop</u>.

Every sentence must contain a verb. There are four main types of sentences:

- <u>statements</u>

- <u>questions</u>

- <u>command sentences</u>

- <u>exclamations</u>

(See also <u>simple</u>, <u>compound</u> and <u>complex sentences</u>.)

SERIAL (seer-re-al) A <u>story</u> which is told, viewed or heard in a <u>sequence</u> of separate parts each contributing to the order of the story through a connected series of events. A serial may be long running, e.g. *a <u>soap opera</u>* or *a set number of episodes*.

SERIES (seer-eez) A set of programmes produced usually for television or radio which are self-contained and independent but with each one following a <u>theme</u> that is common to them all.

SETTING Where the <u>plot</u> for a <u>story</u> happens, e.g. *the setting for a story about Tarzan is the jungle.*

SEQUENCE (see-kw-ens) The way that <u>writing</u> proceeds in order, from start to finish.

SHAPE POEM (See Concrete Poem.)

SHORT STOP (See Punctuation Mark.)

SHORT STORY A short piece of <u>prose</u> <u>fiction</u> usually between 2000-20000 words and which can usually be read at one sitting. Short stories tend to be less complex than <u>novellas</u> or <u>novels</u> and usually focus on only one incident or have a single <u>plot</u>, a single <u>setting</u> and few <u>characters</u>. They are also more concise and to the point than novellas or novels.

SHORT STORY STRUCTURE (Also see Story Structure.) A <u>short story</u> may not have an <u>exposition</u> but have instead an abrupt beginning with the <u>story</u> starting in the middle of the action. They may have a <u>climax</u>, <u>crisis</u> or turning point. Endings may be abrupt and open and may or may not have a <u>moral</u> or <u>practical lesson</u>.

SHORTENED WORD (See Contraction.)

SILENT LETTERS <u>Letters</u> in <u>words</u> that are not pronounced. They can appear at the beginning, middle or end of words.

	<u>word</u>	<u>pronounced</u>	<u>missing</u>
beginning	knife	nife	k
middle	listen	lissen	t
end	autumn	autum	n

SIMILAR WORDS (Also see Synonym.) <u>Words</u> that have roughly the same meaning. They can be used interchangeably to express ideas that are much the same, e.g. *velocity/speed, courageous/brave, jump/leap*.

SIMILE (sim-uh-lee) A comparison which uses the <u>words</u> '*like*' and '*as*'. You can use similes to make your <u>writing</u> more interesting and exciting.

Don drove *like a maniac.*

Mary was *as good as gold.*

The moon was *like a lump of yellow cheese.*

SIMPLE SENTENCE (sim-pul sent-ens) has only one <u>subject</u> and one <u>predicate</u>. (Also see Clause.)

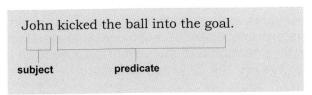

SINGULAR (sing-gu-lar) <u>Words</u> that refer to one thing or one group of things, e.g. *a man/a group of men, a sheep/a flock of sheep, a fly/ a swarm of flies*. (See also <u>Plural</u>.)

SINGULAR NOUN (sing-gu-lar nown) (See Noun.)

SITUATIONAL IRONY (sit-u-a-shun-al i-ron-ee) When an event occurs which is not only unexpected but is also the opposite of what might have been expected or appropriate.

> In *'To Kill a Mockingbird'* by Nellie Harper Lee, Jem and Scout are saved by Boo Radley who had ironically been an object of fear and suspicion to them at the beginning of the novel.

SKIM READING A way of reading quickly to save time and effort. Skim reading gives a general understanding of what a <u>text</u> is about but will not inform in detail about it.

SLANG (See Non-standard English.)

SLOGAN (slow-gen) A catchy, easily remembered <u>phrase</u> which reminds you of a product shown in an advertisement, e.g. *"Tasty, Tasty, very very Tasty"*. Slogans often use <u>rhyme</u> and <u>alliteration</u> to create impact.

SOAP OPERA (sope op-a-ra) A production for television or radio which presents imaginary or fantasy situations and characters as if they were real. Soap operas are shown in serial sequence with each episode continuing the story from the previous episode. Soap operas are characterised by storylines that often feature cliffhanger endings between episodes to keep the audience interested.

SOLILOQUY (soh-lil-oh-kwee) A speech made by a character alone on stage and speaking directly to the audience, the aim being to explain what the character is thinking and to disclose their innermost thoughts.

In Shakespeare's play 'Hamlet', Hamlet begins his soliloquy with the words "To be or not to be".

SONG A relatively brief composition performed to music and sung by the human voice. The words of a song are called lyrics and they may be of a poetic or rhyming nature.

SONNET A poem with fourteen lines and with a clear rhyme scheme. William Shakespeare wrote some famous sonnets.

Who will believe my verse in time to come,
If it were fill'd with your most high deserts?
Though yet heaven knows, it is but as a tomb
Which hides your life, and shows not half your parts.
If I could write the beauty of your eyes,
And in fresh numbers number all your graces,
The age to come would say 'This poet lies,
Such heavenly touches ne'er touch'd earthly faces.'
So should my papers, yellowed with their age,
Be scorn'd, like old men of less truth than tongue,
And your true rights be term'd a poet's rage,
And stretched metre of an antique song:
  But were some child of yours alive that time,
  You should live twice, in it and in my rhyme.
                    by William Shakespeare

SOUND PATTERN The sounds made when <u>words</u> share the same <u>vowel</u> sounds. (See Assonance.)

SPEECH MARKS (Also known as inverted commas, quotes or quotation marks.) They are <u>punctuation marks</u> (" ") put at the start and end of the <u>words</u> that are actually spoken. They appear like the numbers 66 and 99 (only much smaller!).

SPELLING The accepted way <u>letters</u> are written within a <u>word</u>.

SPIDERGRAM A spider shaped diagram (resembling a spider's body and legs) that is used as a tool to help planning, for example during <u>mind mapping</u> or a <u>brainstorm</u> or a <u>thought shower</u>.

A central box contains the idea/topic being considered. Information relating to the topic is noted down in boxes connected to the central box by radiating lines.

It can also be used during revision for an exam or to plan an essay.

SPLIT INFINITIVE (split in-fin-it-iv) When an <u>adverb</u> or <u>phrase</u> comes between "to" and the rest of the <u>verb</u>, e.g. to *badly* need, to *carefully* look. Using split infinitives is considered incorrect English and should be avoided.

> 'to go boldly' not 'to boldly go'
>
> 'to write neatly' not 'to neatly write'
>
> 'to run quickly' not 'to quickly run'

Nowadays, writers and speakers tend to rely on the way the <u>sentence</u> sounds and whether it communicates effectively a sense of meaning, rather than applying an arbitrary rule.

SPOONERISM (spoon-er-riz-um) The mixing up of the initial sounds of two or more words to produce an amusing result.

spoonerism	intended meaning
A well boiled icicle	A well oiled bicycle
Let me sew you to your seat.	Let me show you to your seat.
It is kisstomary to cuss the bride.	It is customary to kiss the bride.
Go and shake a tower.	Go and take a shower.

STAGE DIRECTION (st-ayj di-reck-shun) The detail written as a part of a play script that shows what the actors do, when to come in and when to leave the stage.

Stage directions are written in brackets and provide all the background details about who does what.

STANDARD ENGLISH The kind of formal language we use in writing. It is used in business, education and government and in most books. (Contrast with Non-Standard English.)

STANZA (stan-zar) The structure of the poem usually consists of a number of stanzas. Each stanza is made up of two to four or more usually rhymed lines. The pattern of syllables and rhyming is the same for all stanzas in a poem. The lines of the stanza may also be called verses.

STATEMENT A sentence which states a fact, e.g. *It is very cold.*

STORY (staw-ree) A narrative, either true or fictitious, in prose or verse, designed to interest, entertain or inform the reader or hearer. In longer forms of fiction, stories tend to contain certain core elements of dramatic structure.

STORYBOARD (staw-ree bord) A series of drawings or sketches that set out in sequence the <u>scenes</u> to be shot in a film or video. Each picture shows a major change of action or <u>plot</u> in the production.

STORYLINE (staw-ree-line) (Also known as a Plotline.) In a <u>story</u> or <u>drama</u> the storyline comprises the <u>narrative</u> threads experienced by different <u>characters</u> that together form a <u>plot</u> or <u>subplot</u> in a work of <u>fiction</u>.

STORY STRUCTURE (staw-ree struck-chur) Longer forms of <u>fiction</u> stories tend to follow a structure in which the various elements of a <u>story</u> are arranged. This typically follows a pattern of:

- <u>exposition</u>
- <u>complication</u>
- <u>conflict</u>
- <u>rising action</u>
- <u>crisis</u>
- <u>climax</u>
- <u>falling action</u>
- <u>denouement/resolution</u>
- <u>moral</u> or <u>practical lesson</u>

STRAPLINE (Also known as a <u>Catchline</u> or <u>Tagline</u>.) A simple and catchy <u>phrase</u> or <u>sentence</u> which appears as a secondary <u>statement</u> accompanying a logo or brand name. It is directly linked to the product and usually states something very positive about the product.

The purpose of a strapline is to emphasise a phrase that the company wishes to be remembered by and which, when well established over a long period, becomes an important part of its image.

Barbon Honey Producers	(Company)
Bee the Best!	(Strapline)
Murray and Ross Auto Traders	(Company)
Deals on Wheels	(Strapline)

STRUCTURE (struck-chur) The manner in which the various elements of a <u>story</u> or <u>poem</u> are put together. In a simple structure most stories would have a beginning, middle and end. (See also Story Structure.)

STYLE OF WRITING (st-ile of ri-ting) The way the writer has written to address a particular <u>audience</u>. This may involve techniques such as long descriptive <u>sentence</u>s (in <u>novels</u>), short sentences to create suspense (in horror and thrillers), interesting descriptive sentences (in brochures), <u>rhetorical questions</u> (in speeches), <u>etc</u>.

Style is also the way an <u>author</u> uses words to create a distinctive manner of expression and it is a principal means by which one writer's work is distinguished from another.

SUBHEADING (sub-hed-ing) A general or descriptive heading for a section of written work used within the <u>context</u> of a main <u>story</u> or <u>article</u>. A subheading provides a way of dividing up a longer piece of <u>text</u> into shorter parts and it indicates what the passage below is about.

SUBJECT (sub-jeckt) The part of a <u>sentence</u> which tells you the person or thing that the sentence is about.

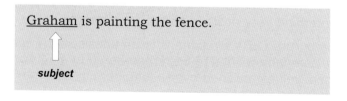

<u>Graham</u> is painting the fence.

subject

SUBJECT AND VERB AGREEMENT In a <u>sentence</u> the <u>subject</u> and <u>verb</u> must "agree with" or match each other.

- ◆ When the subject is <u>singular</u> the verb used with it should also be singular.

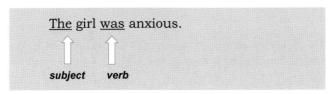

- ◆ When the subject is <u>plural</u> the plural form of the verb should be used.

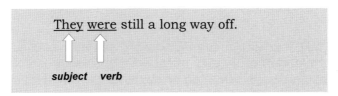

SUBORDINATE CLAUSE (sub-ord-in-ate clors) (See Clause. Also known as a Dependent Clause.)

SUBPLOT A secondary <u>plot</u> that occurs alongside the main plot in a <u>play</u>, <u>novel</u> or other <u>literary</u> work.

In 'Twelfth Night' by William Shakespeare, the subplot is concerned with Sir Toby Belch and Sir Andrew Aguecheek making a fool out Malvolio.

SUBTEXT The hidden meanings not clearly stated by the writer in the <u>text</u>. These messages can be communicated to the reader as an overall impression of what has been read. Although not stated, the reader is left with a distinct impression and understanding of the writer's intended <u>viewpoint</u>.

SUBTITLE (sub-ti-tal) A secondary, alternate and usually explanatory <u>title</u> that accompanies a <u>literary</u> work, whether it be a <u>book</u>, film, <u>play</u> or musical work, <u>etc</u>.

It also means a written translation of a foreign-<u>language</u> film shown at the bottom of the screen.

SUFFIX A letter or group of <u>letters</u> added to the end of a word to change the way it is used.

> love   ⇒   love*ly*
>
> mop   ⇒   mop*ping*
>
> hot   ⇒   hot*ter*

SUGGEST (su-jest) A <u>command word</u> sometimes used in an examination or <u>literacy</u> <u>question</u>. This requires you to consider the information or evidence pertinent to the question and make a judgement. Then put forward a suggestion with an idea or reason to support the judgement that has been made.

SUPERLATIVE (soo-per-la-tiv) (See Adjective.)

SYLLABLE (sill-a-bul) A part of a word pronounced as a single sound. A syllable can form a complete word.

word	No of syllables
cat	1
wa-ter	2
won-der-ful	3
cat-er-pill-ar	4

Syllables usually consist of a <u>vowel</u> sound with or without the <u>consonant</u> sounds that are attached to it, whether preceding or following the vowel.

SYLLABLE PATTERNS (sill-a-bul pat-turns) Used in <u>poem</u>s so that each line has a set number of <u>syllable</u>s. This gives the <u>poem</u> a <u>structure</u> and <u>rhythm</u> that can be read easily.

SYMBOL (sim-bul) A representation using an image or <u>word</u> to represent a group, an idea or an object.

symbol	meaning
heart	love
lion	courage or strength
hawk	war
dove	peace

SYMBOLISM (sim-bul-ism) The applied use of specific objects or images to represent abstract ideas. These would be recognisable iconic representations that carry meanings that are widely understood.

symbol	meaning
a set of scales	justice
red cross	medical aid and food relief

SYNTAX (sin-tacks) The way that <u>word</u>s are arranged to create <u>sentence</u>s.

SYNONYM (sin-oh-nim) (Also see Similar Words) A <u>word</u> that has a similar meaning to another word. These are useful words if you want to describe the same thing twice and you want to avoid repeating yourself.

halt	⟹	stop
gather	⟹	collect
small	⟹	little
liberty	⟹	freedom

SYNOPSIS (sin-op-sis) A summary of a <u>text</u> that tells you the main events of the <u>story</u> in a shortened form.

TABLEAUX (tab-low) (Also known as a Freeze Frame.) A representation of a <u>scene</u> created by arranging a group of people in a particular way and in appropriate postures while remaining silent and motionless. The silent picture can portray a moment in time, an event, an idea or even a memory.

Tableaux is a useful dramatic technique to create an impression more powerful than through <u>word</u>s alone.

TABLOID WRITING (tab-loy-d ri-ting) (Also see Newspaper.) A <u>style of writing</u> and reporting, used in a newspaper, that sets out to represent popular culture. It is characterised by:

- sensational stories

- big, bold and often humorous <u>headline</u>s

- an accessible and basic <u>language</u> level

- <u>biase</u>d and emotional language

- short news <u>article</u>s that often mix fact and opinion

- a focus on reporting events in the lives of well known personalities

- a style of writing that is easy to read

Examples of <u>newspapers</u> written in a tabloid style are The Sun, The Daily Star, The Daily Mirror.

TAGLINE (See Strapline. Also known as a Catchline.)

TALE (tayl) A <u>narrative</u> that tells the detail of a course of real or imaginary events. This may be presented in <u>writing</u> or <u>drama</u> or cinema, or as a radio or television programme.

TANKA (tang-ker) A <u>haiku</u> <u>poem</u> with two or more seven <u>syllable</u> lines added to give more of a picture of the subject the poem is describing.

TAUTOLOGY (tort-ol-o-gee) The use of an extra word or phrase which pointlessly repeats an idea already expressed in a sentence.

> The *weekly* newsletter is written *each week*.
>
> He decided to *return* the book *back* to the library.
>
> Platina made a *beeline straight* here.

TENSE The verb tense shows the time when an action takes place. (The word tense comes from the Latin word "tempus" meaning time.) There are three main tenses, Present Tense, Past Tense and Future Tense.

> Today I *go* to school.   [present tense]
>
> Yesterday I *went* to school   [past tense]
>
> Tomorrow I *will go* to school   [future tense]

(Nb. Beginner writers often find it best to write in the past tense as that is easier to sustain.)

TEXT Any kind of writing. Written text would include novels, instructions, stories, letters and articles.

TEXT ANALYSIS (text an-al-eh-sis) A process used to find out more about a text. Two acronyms are helpful to focus the approach.

> **G**enre (Text type)   **P**urpose
>
> **A**udience   **A**udience
>
> **P**urpose   **T**ext type (Genre)

> The above acronyms spell the words **GAP** and **PAT**. You can remember them by "**PAT** the text" and "mind the **GAP**".

- Genre – what type of text is this?

- Audience – who is the text aimed at?

- Purpose – what sort of response is the text expecting from the reader, e.g. *to persuade, entertain or inform*?

To analyse a text further, apply an approach such as:

> *L*anguage
>
> *I*nformation
>
> *S*tyle
>
> *T*one
>
> (The above is an acronym. You can remember the points because they spell ***LIST***)

- Language – is this descriptive, informative, persuasive? Is an emotional response produced in the reader?

- Information – is this factual, imaginary, the writer's opinion or a mixture of all three?

- Style – how is the text presented? The format used, e.g. *leaflet, poster* or *novel*. How the text is written, e.g. *short paragraphs, bullet points* or *related to illustrations*.

- Tone – this is linked to the language used, e.g. *serious, humorous, sad* or *angry*. How would it sound if read aloud?

When producing a text analysis using this approach, a student would be expected to provide evidence/give examples for each part.

TEXT LANGUAGE (text lang-gwi-dge) An informal, personal and abbreviated language used in text messages on mobile phones. A language convention which is only acceptable when used in sending text messages.

THEATRE (th-ee-a-ter) A building or place where dramatised events are enacted. A place where plays and shows are presented or performed for the entertainment of an audience.

THEME (th-ee-m) What a poem, story, novel, film or play is about. The subject or subjects covered, not just the facts but the ideas and thinking behind the facts, e.g. *the theme of most crime novels is about the committing, investigating and solving of a crime.*

The themes of great works of literature are often different to the plot, e.g. *The plot of William Shakespeare's play "The Tempest", is about a shipwreck on a desert island;* its themes are to do with power and authority.

THESIS (thee-sez) An essay or dissertation written upon a specific theme and proposing an original point of view as an outcome of research. A thesis may be a requirement of a diploma or degree course.

A thesis is also a proposition stated or put forward for consideration, discussion and argument.

THIRD PERSON The form of a pronoun and/or verb used to refer to something or someone other than the speaker or the person or people being addressed, e.g. in English, the pronoun *"she", "he", "it"* (all singular) and *"they"* (plural) are used.

It is also the style of writing used when the story is written about someone else.

He walked down the road.

She typed on the computer.

They went to the match.

THOUGHT SHOWER (th-ort shou-er) (Also known as Brainstorm or Mind-mapping.) The process of generating new ideas through discussion of a particular topic, subject or event.

THOUGHT TRACKING (th-ort tr-ack-ing) A <u>drama</u> convention where the inner thoughts of individuals are shared.

It is appropriate to use thought tracking at particular points in a drama to focus on individual <u>characters</u> so that their thoughts, views and opinions can be expressed. Either the character themselves or another person can 'speak' the character's thoughts.

TITLE (ti-tal) An identifying name given to a <u>book</u>, <u>play</u>, film or other written work. A general descriptive heading that informs the reader/viewer/listener about the item that follows.

The convention for using <u>capital letter</u>s in a <u>title</u> is to put them at the start of the important words. Lower case <u>letters</u> are used for the short words.

> The *L*ion, the *W*itch and the *W*ardrobe
>
> The *W*izard of *O*z
>
> *F*ive go to *M*ystery *M*oor

TONE (to-own) The way in which words are used to create a <u>mood</u> or feeling about what is happening in a <u>poem</u> or <u>story</u>. It can best be considered when asking yourself what tone of voice you would use if reading the story or poem aloud.

> *The poem has a bitter, mocking tone revealing the narrator's anger and resentment.*

TONGUE-TWISTER (tung tw-is-ta) Amusing sayings or <u>rhyme</u>s that use lots of similar <u>consonant</u> sounds so that it is difficult to say them quickly.

> *She sells sea shells on the sea shore.*
> *Around the rugged rocks the ragged rascal ran.*

TRADITIONAL TALE (trad-ish-un-al tay-l) A well known <u>story</u> that is written, read and told in all cultures. The stories follow a similar pattern and often involve a <u>theme</u> of good against evil. (Also see Legend and Fairy Tale.)

TRAGEDY (trag-ed-ee) A <u>drama</u> or <u>literary</u> word typically describing the downfall of a great person. This may involve a <u>protagonist</u> who is strong-willed but has a tragic flaw such as moral weakness or the inability to cope with unfavourable circumstances, in a <u>conflict</u> with a superior force such as destiny.

A tragedy can also be a drama, usually a play, where people die at the end, e.g. *'Romeo and Juliet'* and *'Macbeth'* by William Shakespeare.

TRANSCRIPT (trans-sk-ript) Something that has been transcribed. Usually a written or type-written record of dictated or recorded speech.

> He read a *transcript* of the prisoner's interrogation.
>
> Write to us at the radio station to receive a *transcript* of her radio interview.

TWIST IN THE TALE (Also known as a Plot Twist.) A technique used by writers to make a <u>story</u> take a change of direction that is unexpected and would not have been predicted by the reader.

UNDERSTATEMENT (See Meiosis.)

UPPER CASE LETTERS (See Alphabet.)

VERBAL IRONY (ver-bal i-ron-ee) An expression in which what is said and what is intended is the opposite of what the <u>words</u> literally mean.

> A small reward for a great amount of work may be greeted by the words, *"Thanks a lot!"*

When accompanied by a <u>tone</u> of voice that emphasises disapproval or scorn, verbal irony becomes <u>sarcasm</u>.

VERBOSITY (ver-boss-it-ee) Using too many <u>words</u> to express something so that the meaning becomes confused and unclear.

VERB PHRASE (See Phrase.)

VERB is a **doing** or **action** word. Verbs tell you what a person or thing is doing, e.g. *walking, climbing, playing.*

Sometimes verbs are not actually physical actions but they are still verbs, e.g. *to wish, to think, to try.*

Verbs can also be **being** words that show us what something is, e.g. *was, were, will be, am, are, is.*

A verb is the most important word in a <u>sentence</u>. Without a verb a sentence would not make sense.

Verbs can be single words. Sometimes a verb is made up of more than one word to show a different time or <u>tense</u> like past, present or future. (See Root Verb.)

> Alice *was helping* her mum.
>
> Evie *is going* out to play.

- **Auxiliary** verbs are "helper" verbs which help the main verb to work properly.

> Peter *was* hoping for a goal soon.

- **Negative** verbs are formed by adding 'not' after the auxiliary verb.

> 'have closed' becomes 'have *not* closed'
>
> 'can read' becomes 'can*not* read'

- **Active** verbs are when the <u>subject</u> of the <u>sentence</u> is doing the action.

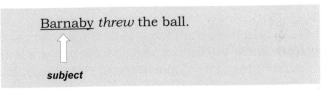

Active verbs are stronger and more direct. They are also shorter and easier to read. They can be used to make <u>writing</u> more lively and exciting.

- **Passive** verbs are used when the <u>subject</u> of the sentence is having something done to it or him or her. Passive verbs such as *is, was, will be* are used with the verb.

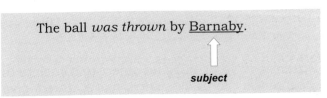

Passive verbs are often used in public notices because they sound less aggressive and abrupt than the active verbs.

> *No running allowed*   [active]
>
> is more hostile than:
>
> *Running is not allowed*   [passive]

They are used in <u>report</u> writing, in science experiments or to conceal who was responsible.

> *The vase was broken.*　　[passive]
>
> instead of:
>
> *Mary broke the vase.*　　[active]

- **Finite verbs** are those which show tense, person or <u>singular/plural</u> status, e.g. *He walks, She swam, They cooked.*

- **Non-finite verbs** are less specific and are without person, tense or singular/plural status, e.g. *to walk, to improve.*

- **Modal verbs** convey ideas like intention, possibility, obligation and/or necessity, e.g. *can, could, would, will, ought to, need to, must.*

- **Transitive** verbs take the action from the <u>subject</u> across to the <u>object</u>.

> Dogs *chase* cats.
>
> Connor *washed* his face.

Transitive verbs need an <u>object</u> to complete the sentence. Verbs like *catch, make, asked, give, find* and *do* should all have an object.

- **Intransitive** verbs do not need an object as they make sense on their own.

> The clock *ticks.*
>
> Your socks *smell.*

- **Regular** verbs are the main part of the verb and stay the same when the tense changes.

Present tense	Past tense
I *chew* gum.	I *chewed* gum.
I *climb* trees.	I *climbed* trees.

- **Irregular** verbs change the main part of the verb when the tense changes.

Present tense	Past tense
I *buy* shoes.	I *bought* shoes.
I *run* to school.	I *ran* to school.

- **Interrogative** verb forms are used to ask <u>questions</u> by changing the word order.

> Alice *was annoying* William.
>
> becomes:
>
> *Was* Alice *annoying* William?

- **Imperative** verbs are when the <u>second person</u> form (you) is left off in a sentence.

> You *chase* it.
>
> becomes:
>
> *Chase* it.

- **'To be'** is the most common verb in the English <u>language</u>. We use the verb 'is' when we are talking about one thing or person.

> The girl *is* running.

We use 'are' or 'were' when we are talking about more than one thing or person.

The girls *were* running.

Present tense	Past tense
is	was
are	were

VERB TENSE There are six common types of Verb Tense: <u>Past Tense</u>, <u>Present Tense</u> , <u>Future Tense</u> , <u>Past Perfect Tense</u>, <u>Present Perfect Tense</u> and <u>Future Perfect Tense</u>. (Also see Conjugation.)

Six Verb Tenses		
Past Tense	Present Tense	Future Tense
Past Perfect Tense	Present Perfect Tense	Future Perfect Tense

VERSE A section of a <u>poem</u>, or an expression in words which conforms to accepted rules of <u>metre</u> and <u>structure</u>. A group of lines that follow the same pattern, i.e. similar number of words, <u>rhyme</u> and <u>syllable pattern</u>.

VOCABULARY (vo-cab-yu-la-ree) The main <u>words</u> used in a <u>language</u>. These can be listed in a <u>dictionary</u> or <u>lexicon</u> in <u>alphabetical order</u> with meanings given.

VOWEL (vou-el) Five <u>letters</u> of the <u>alphabet</u> are vowels: *A,E,I,O,U (a,e,i,o,u)*. Every English word contains at least one vowel. Sometimes '*y*' is used as a vowel, in words like *my, fly, try* and *rhyme*.

WIT The clever and original use of words and expressions to make connections and associations between ideas to achieve a humorous result.

> *"If there is no money in poetry, neither is there poetry in money."* Rupert Graves (1895-1995) British poet.
>
> *"Wit ought to be a glorious treat like caviar. Never spread it about like marmalade."* Noel Coward

WORD A group of <u>letters</u> which when arranged together has a specific grammatical function or meaning and is recognised as a <u>part of speech</u>.

WRITING (rye-ting) A way of expressing ideas using a written format to create or form characters, letters and words, usually in a meaningful way, to constitute readable material. Writing is created on the surface of some material such as paper using a device for recording such as a pen, pencil, typewriter, keyboard/word processor.

Writing is a principal means of communicating thoughts and ideas with others.

WRITING IN ROLE (rye-ting in roll) Opportunities for different types of <u>writing</u> can emerge from or be the precursor to different types of <u>drama</u>. <u>Letter</u>s, messages, diaries, <u>notes</u> and <u>graffiti</u> can all be different writing <u>genre</u>s expressed by the <u>character</u>s.

ZEUGMA (zoog-muh) A <u>figure of speech</u> which uses <u>word</u> association to convey emotion and <u>mood</u> often in a non-literal sense. Zeugma is the use of a word to modify or govern two or more words in such a way that it applies to each in a different sense.

He *lost* his coat and his temper.

She *opened* her door and her heart to the orphan.

The addict *kicked* the habit and then the bucket.

He *caught* two fish and a cold.